Penguin Handbooks
Modern Vegetarian Cookery

Walter and Jenny Fliess were both born in Germany and owned two vegetarian restaurants in Cologne. They emigrated to England in 1933 where they became well known as the founders and working owners of the internationally reputed Vega Restaurant in London's Leicester Square. Their autograph book is packed with the names of famous politicians, writers, actors, sportsmen, and others, and altogether they served more than five million meals 'without a casualty'.

Jenny Fliess got her training under Dr O. M. Bircher-Benner at his famous sanatorium in Switzerland. Walter Fliess studied restaurant management in the U.S.A. In 1954 at Hotelympia he won in the vegetarian class the silver challenge trophy and gold medal for culinary art.

Both travelled widely, and gathered recipes for new vegetarian dishes on four continents. This book contains, in compressed form, a good slice of their lives' work.

Modern Vegetarian Cookery was awarded a bronze medal by the Gastronomische Akademie Deutschlands in 1968.

Walter and Jenny Fliess

Modern Vegetarian Cookery

Penguin Books

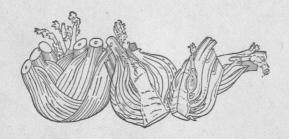

Penguin Books Ltd, Harmondsworth, Middlesex, England
Viking Penguin Inc., 40 West 23rd Street, New York, New York 10010, U.S.A.
Penguin Books Australia Ltd, Ringwood, Victoria, Australia
Penguin Books Canada Ltd, 2801 John Street, Markham, Ontario, Canada L3R 1B4
Penguin Books (N.Z.) Ltd, 182–190 Wairau Road, Auckland 10, New Zealand

First published 1964
Reprinted 1965, 1968, 1970, 1971, 1972, 1973, 1974, 1975, 1976,
1977 (twice), 1978, 1979, 1980, 1981, 1982, 1983, 1984, 1985

Made and printed in Great Britain by
Hazell Watson & Viney Limited,
Member of the BPCC Group,
Aylesbury, Bucks
Set in Monotype Ehrhardt

Drawings by Mary Waldron

Contents

Foreword

Culinary art is as old as human civilization. But recent research in the field of nutrition, together with the anxiety many people feel about the increasing use of chemicals in agriculture and food processing, has led to a reappraisal of old habits, and new ideas have come to the fore.

The results of all this are neither complete nor universally agreed upon. However, in this book we are little concerned with theories. We feel the time has come to help the harassed house-wife, if she wants to change, for a short or a long period, to a different diet in which the advice 'plenty of fresh vegetables and fruit' is the dominant feature. Whether this advice has come from the doctor or friends or from the 'keep fit' and slimming columns of the magazines, the usual reaction has been one of bewilderment. Little do people realize how attractive and excit-ing such a régime can be.

We have been in charge of vegetarian restaurants for over twenty-five years, and early turned our attention to the numerous uses of all the wonderful vegetables available. On the Continent, when talking about English cooking, we used to say 'Those poor English, they only know three vegetables and two of them are cabbage.' This is true no more. Not only is there now a much larger variety of home-grown produce – even artichokes, celeriac, salsify, sea kale, and corn cobs are being grown com-mercially in this country – but, thanks to refrigeration and air transport, the fruits and vegetables of tropical and sub-tropical regions are also available. Such 'strange' vegetables as green peppers and aubergines are now a common sight at the better greengrocers. But how many people know how to use them?

There are a hundred and one different ways of cooking, from austere boiling – now somewhat obsolete – through a whole range of more sophisticated methods to the elaborate but delicious Chinese ways. In this book we have tried to give examples from the whole range – the greatest possible variety of recipes, together with suggestions for combining them into delicious and nourishing meals.

FOREWORD TO THIS EDITION

Since this book was first published in 1964 a chapter on Quantities, Weights and Measures (pp. 17 and 18) has been added, together with a simplified Conversion Table. This has proved very useful when the metric system or cup measures are used. Instructions have also been added to explain when it is necessary to follow the quantities given in the recipes strictly, or when it is safe to vary quantities to suit personal preference.

Thanks to some observant users of the book who have kindly written to us, a few minor inaccuracies have been corrected. The opportunity has been taken to revise the book throughout, to ensure that it remains as fully contemporary as the first edition.

How to make the best use of this book

This book can be used either as a straightforward handbook for its recipes, or as a full course in modern vegetarian cookery. The recipes are all described in enough detail for anyone with only a little cooking experience to be able to follow them; and we have tried to anticipate, and provide remedies for, any snags which seem likely.

The brief chapter on Quantities (page 17) should be read by all; those who want a change of diet should read the introductions to the different sections, which are short but constructive, particularly the ones on Uncooked Dishes (page 168) and Menu Suggestions (page 225). If you follow the simple rules prescribed, calories and food values will look after themselves, and you can concentrate on trying out new ideas on your family. You will soon find out how easy it is.

COOL FOOD FOR HOT SEASONS

The height of summer is a good time to change, for at least some meals, to an uncooked diet with all the benefit this entails. It gives you the chance to introduce interesting salads, some of which may be so highly appreciated that they will become part of the normal routine on colder days too. In particular, the cold fruit soups (pages 32–6) have proved extremely popular during the summer months.

FOR THE OCCASIONAL GUEST ON A SPECIAL DIET

This need not be an embarrassing situation, even if it arises at short notice. The common mistake is to believe that one has

to cook a complete meal for the guest who unexpectedly turns out
to be a vegetarian. Most of the things you have in your larder or
have planned for your own meal (vegetables, the sweet) are
probably vegetarian anyhow. As long as the vegetables are not
mixed up with the gravy, it is only the fish or the meat for which
a substitute must be found. This is easy enough if you go through
the section of main course dishes (pages 116 ff.) and select a dish
for which the ingredients are at hand; the section on quick
savouries (page 160) should be particularly helpful in such cases.

WESTERN DISHES FOR EASTERN VEGETARIANS

A change from the traditional local food to the European-
style meals is often a side issue to the introduction of Western
techniques and ideals in developing countries. This is for many
Hindus and Buddhists a religious problem, for they think – quite
mistakenly – that European style is synonymous with a meat-
eating way of life. We hope they will find in this book examples
of Western dishes they can enjoy without compromising their
beliefs. Eggs and some other ingredients may not be permissible
for certain sects but there are plenty of dishes and recipes in this
book without them.

Special kitchen implements

There are no special implements required for modern vegetarian or food reform cookery. Good saucepans, preferably of stainless steel, one or two heavy frying pans, a casserole dish, and a few fireproof dishes are useful in any kitchen. The latter, however, are a must. They can be made of glass, enamelled cast iron, or earthenware; some are 'flameproof', others only 'ovenproof', that is, not to be put on an open flame.

For salads, a few mixing bowls and a couple of graters, one fine, one coarse, are all that is required. A good grater should have proper perforation; not only sharp edges for the actual shredding but also proper holes to allow the material to get through. An excellent one is the Swiss Dr Bircher grater, made of stainless steel. Similar but cheap ones may not last so long but are equally good if their perforation is a fair copy of the original. There are also some small rotary graters with a handle (such as the 'Mouli' grater) which are particularly useful for grating cheese and nuts.

Another useful piece of equipment is a simple strainer with blades rotated by a handle (a 'Mouli-légumes') to rub vegetables or fruit through a sieve. They are now available in all good hardware stores. For juice extractors see page 205.

Otherwise we have found that the usefulness of many gadgets, in particular electrical ones, is rather overrated, as far as the small family is concerned, when one makes allowance for the time taken for assembling, cleaning, and so on. For the larger family, however, the modern universal mixing machine can be a great help. When buying one, make sure it is really strong and has a mincer and shredding attachment.

Notes on raw materials

FATS AND OILS

Vegetable fats and oils are obtained mainly from the seeds of plants such as maize, groundnuts, sunflowers, palms, and flax. Olive oil is somewhat different as it is obtained from the fleshy part of the olive. The best quality is from the first (cold) pressing; cheaper ones are usually chemically or steam extracted. Fats and oils differ in degree rather than in kind. Fats are hard at ordinary room temperatures, but even some oils can get hard on cold days.

Current medical opinion prefers the more fluid 'unsaturated' fats and oils to the harder, saturated ones which have a higher proportion of hydrogen. Sunflower and corn (maize) oils are some of the best unsaturated ones. Apart from olive oil which has its own special flavour, all oils taste neutral these days as they are processed and deodorized.

There are good vegetarian margarines on the market (Tomor, Golden Block, Gala, and others); these are made exclusively from vegetable oil and are guaranteed to contain no fish or any other animal fat. They all contain a small proportion of water and some vegetable oils chemically hardened by hydrogenation. White fats such as Trex, Suenut, etc. contain practically no water. When 'fat' is specified in our recipes it does not matter which type is used.

Butter, of course, is excellent for cooking. It contains a certain amount of water, and a proportion of naturally occurring saturated fat. In the few cases where we specify butter as an ingredient, it is mainly because of its flavour, and margarine *can* be used in its place.

Oil kept for deep frying loses its 'strength' after a certain amount of use. It will regain its strength when 'rested' for two to three weeks, but it should be strained first.

MILK

Your dairy will willingly explain the different types of milk available. Most milks are treated in some way. They may be pasteurized, that is, heated so that germs are killed, and/or homogenized – the fat globules broken down, to prevent the cream separating from the milk. Some people prefer unpasteurized milk, considering it a more natural product, but for cooking it really does not matter, as the milk will be exposed to heat anyhow.

Yoghourt is rich milk which has become sour and fairly solid by fermentation with the special yoghourt culture (*bacillus bulgaricus*).

Milk substitutes from plants may become available in the not too distant future. At present only small quantities are manufactured for special purposes.

CHEESE

Parmesan cheese, old, hard, and expensive, is the best for grating and cooking. But good-quality Cheddar or Cheshire, not too fresh, is almost as good, and much cheaper. Curd cheese and cream cheeses too are excellent from a nutritional point of view; they should be used for cooking where indicated. They are also useful as additions to salads and as salad dressing. Processed cheese or cheese spreads are useless for cooking purposes. They contain little real cheese, too much water and too many additives which may spoil the dish.

EGGS

Most eggs sold at present are from batteries where the chickens are kept in confined spaces and fed 'scientifically'. They are not necessarily better than fresh farm eggs from chickens which have more space and can scratch freely. On the contrary: as battery eggs have a tendency to pale yolks which are unpopular, synthetic dyes are sometimes added to the battery feed to produce the deeper-coloured yolk normally associated with open range feeding.

If you prefer not to use eggs at all, soya flour is usually the best substitute. Some recipes for this are given in the book, but as methods of milling the soya beans differ widely, the soya flour too varies in its composition, and it is recommended that the instructions issued with the flour should be followed.

VEGETABLES AND FRUIT

These are the main providers of important nutritive elements and vitamin C, the 'protective' vitamin, but freshness is vitally important. We do not wish to enter here the controversy about the use of chemical fertilizers and sprays. One thing, however, is beyond doubt: certain vegetables, such as celery, lettuce, and tomatoes, taste much better if 'compost-grown', that is, without chemical treatment. Fruit is normally sprayed with toxic insecticides and these substances are sometimes mixed with fixing agents to prevent them from being washed off by the rain. To be sure that they are removed, wash fruit very thoroughly, preferably in warm water, or, to be quite sure, peel it. This is, of course, a pity as some fruit skins contain valuable minerals. If orange or lemon rind is to be used, the fruit should first be properly scrubbed or it should be from fruit not dyed or chemically treated.

FLOUR

More and more people are turning to wholemeal bread for their day-to-day use, that is, bread made from flour which contains the whole wheat or rye berry including husk and germ. It contains more protein, more natural vitamins, and more 'roughage' than white flour, which is of lower extraction, finer, and more starchy. Except for pastries, flour is used in our recipes mainly for thickening and binding other ingredients together and for this purpose the starchy flour is easier to use. As the quantities are small we recommend for cooking purposes (as opposed to baking where 100 per cent wholemeal is strongly recommended) a flour known as '81 per cent flour' obtainable in health food stores and good grocers. But if you want to use wholemeal only, this is quite possible if you bear in mind that slightly more flour (or less moisture) is required.

For soya flour see page 13 under Eggs.

PASTA

Noodles, macaroni, spaghetti, vermicelli, and similar products are useful in providing variety for the vegetarian diet. As good-quality pasta is obtainable at all grocers only two recipes – for home-made noodles and ravioli – are given. The others require special implements.

NUTS

All types of nuts, though not cheap, are useful as providers of protein. However, as will be seen from the recipes, they are much less used than is popularly imagined. To enhance the flavour of nuts used for cooking they should be slightly roasted as described in the recipe on page 135.

Note that groundnuts (peanuts) from a nutritional point of view should be classified as leguminous seeds together with peas, beans, and lentils.

SUGAR

Natural brown sugars vary considerably according to the country of origin. All contain a small proportion of salt and other minerals which are absent in white sugar. We have found Barbados sugar the most suitable for all purposes.

In a few recipes 'vanilla sugar' is mentioned. This is ordinary castor sugar kept in a small screw-cap jar with a stick of vanilla from which it absorbs the flavour.

SALT

Only small quantities are needed by the body (except in hot climates where a much larger intake is necessary), and doctors often recommend a saltless diet in cases of over-weight. Alternatives to salt with fancy names are sometimes recommended but we have found that they usually contain a high proportion of ordinary cooking salt. Apart from its nutritional value or otherwise, salt is a valuable flavouring agent; however, it can, if you like, be cut down or even omitted from all our recipes without altering the quantity of the other ingredients. Although the result may be unpalatable at first, it is quite astonishing how quickly one can get used to such a saltless diet, particularly if one increases the use of fresh or dried herbs.

Other synthetic flavourings or flavouring agents such as monosodium glutamate are unnecessary.

VINEGAR

We see no harm in using small quantities of pure malt, cider, or wine vinegar for cooking. Fresh lemon or lime juice can, of course, be used instead. They owe their acidity to a variety of acids and, in addition, contain vitamin C.

YEAST EXTRACTS

Various blends are available: Marmite, Yeastrel, Barmene, Vesop, Maggi, etc., all of which differ slightly in taste, salt content and consistency. They are invaluable in cooking, both for flavouring savoury dishes and as a useful source of the important B vitamins. What is sometimes labelled 'hydrolysed protein' is nothing else but one of various forms of these extracts; it is unlikely to have an animal base.

INSTANT, PROCESSED FOODS AND TVP

A great variety of savoury mixes, dehydrated or tinned meat substitutes, bread spreads and sweets are obtainable in health food shops and some supermarkets. Recently developed as an economical meat substitute with a meaty texture, is TVP (texturized vegetable protein). It is mainly manufactured from the soya bean and/or wheat gluten from which the fat and starch is discarded. No recipes are given in this book for TVP because improvements and changes are still being made. We recommend using the recipes given with each packet.

Quantities, Weights, and Measures

Except for cakes and pastries where weights and measures must be fairly accurate, the quantities given in this book should be considered as of average standard. A gram more or less here and there does not really matter. If you like rich food, slightly increase the fat (and flour) contents, if not, or if you have to watch your weight, decrease it.

Quantities for a given number of persons depend of course on appetite and eating habits. We have assumed that the dishes we describe are part of a substantial three-course meal: Soup, Main Course, and Sweet, where the main course is chosen or adapted from the menu suggestions on pages 225ff. If a recipe is used outside this context, if for instance a Brown Lentil Soup (page 29) is not taken as a first course but as a main dish – which is quite a reasonable thing to do – it is only common sense that the quantities given in the recipe for four to six may in fact be just sufficient for three or four.

ABBREVIATIONS AND CONVERSIONS

With metrication more and more accepted everywhere, the conversion tables on the next page are easy to use for anyone preferring the metric system.

For simplicity's sake we have abandoned mathematical calculations, as for ordinary cooking the tables are sufficiently accurate. As our housewives are probably the last to accept millimetre, gram and litre we are sticking to ounces, pounds and pints. In the U.S.A. and Canada weighing for cooking is frowned upon anyhow. Every household there has a set of measuring cups and measuring spoons. Conversions into these are also in the tables on the next page.

It may be a good idea for those needing the conversions to copy out the relevant part on a small card which then can be used as a bookmark.

British (imperial) measures are used in this book with these abbreviations:

oz. = ounce(s)   Reg. = Regulo no. for
lb. = pound(s)   gas cooker
pt* = pint(s)   tsp. = teaspoon(s)
°   = degree Fahrenheit   Tbs. = tablespoon(s)

*This is the British pint = 20 fluid ounces; the American pint has only 16 fluid ounces.

American Cup and Spoon Measures

American measuring spoons	British measures used in this book 1 lb. = 16 oz.			American measuring cups
all level				*all level*
2 Tbs.	1 oz.	Butter, Fat, Rice, Split Peas, Lentils, Caster Sugar	1 lb.	2 cups
2½ Tbs.	1 oz.	Sugar (granulated)	1 lb.	2½ cups
·3 Tbs.	1 oz.	Flour, Grated Nuts	1 lb.	4 cups
5 Tbs.	1 oz.	Oat Flakes	1 lb.	6 cups
2½ Tbs.	1 oz.	All Liquids, including Oil	1 pt*	2½ cups

*The difference between the British and American pint has been taken care of in the cup measurement.

Weights and Temperatures

British Measure	Metric Equivalent	Oven temperatures	
		°Fahrenheit, used in this book	°Centigrade
1 oz.	30 grams	Slow 300	150
1 lb.	450 grams	Moderate 350	180
1 pt	a little over half litre	Hot 400	210
		Very Hot 450	230

Soups

Soups seem to be coming into fashion again. This is a good thing because they are liked by young and old. If they are home-made and a little trouble is taken over them they can be quite delicious, and they are very cheap. The light soups are excellent appetizers, the more substantial ones are often nourishing enough to be meals in themselves. As they are easy to digest they can be recommended particularly for people when they come home tired from work.

We use, of course, pure vegetable stock (for brevity's sake we call it just 'stock'), and the better the stock the better the soup. Stock is also used for other dishes; but even if no stock is available or you can't be bothered you can still turn out something very palatable.

Quantities. In the soup section all quantities are given for six, i.e. six medium helpings if the soup is just one course of an otherwise substantial meal. If the soup is meant as a meal in itself the given quantities are for three to four persons.

Vegetable Stock. Almost anything in the vegetable line can be used: carrots, not peeled but well scrubbed; cauliflower stalks; outside leaves and stalks of celery and cabbage; vegetable trimmings, etc. Do *not* use: beetroots (they give an unpleasant colour); onions or chicory (their taste is too pronounced); or potatoes (they make the stock cloudy). But otherwise everything. Add water, 2 pts or more according to the amount of vegetables, bring to the boil and simmer for one or two hours. Strain and use the liquid, i.e. the stock, only. The vegetables should by now be quite tasteless and can be thrown away; all the goodness is in the stock.

CLEAR SOUPS (CONSOMMÉS)

Clear Vegetable Broth. For 6

1½ pt stock	1 small bayleaf
½ oz. butter or fat	a few sprigs of parsley
1 tsp. yeast extract	salt to taste

Boil all ingredients except parsley together for about 20 mins., Chop parsley finely and add before serving.

Clear Vegetable Broth Garni

The clear vegetable broth can be garnished and served with:
- (*a*) croûtons ⎫
- (*b*) egg balls ⎬ see below
- (*c*) pancakes cut into narrow strips
- (*d*) small pieces of spaghetti or macaroni
- (*e*) vermicelli or any other pasta suitable for soup.

Croûtons

These are small pieces of bread, preferably wholemeal, fried in plenty of oil or fat until golden brown. They look best if the bread is cut into small cubes just under ½ inch across.

Egg Balls as garnish for soups. For 4 to 6

1 egg	pinch of salt
2 oz. flour	very little grated nutmeg to
2 Tbs. milk	taste

Beat egg, add flour, salt, nutmeg, and lastly the milk. The mixture should be fairly stiff but still runny. Dip a teaspoon into the boiling broth (to prevent the mixture from sticking to it) and then use it to transfer one teaspoonful of the mixture into the broth as a try-out. Boil for 5 mins. without the lid. The egg ball, of irregular shape but still in one piece, should rise to the surface. If the ball falls to pieces, the mixture is not stiff enough, so a little more flour should be added. Then repeat the procedure – not forgetting to dip the teaspoon into the broth before new mixture is transferred. When the whole surface is covered with egg balls take them out and put them aside. Carry on until the mixture is used up. Put the egg balls back into the soup before serving.

Julienne Soup. For 6

1½ pt stock or water	1 small parsnip
1 tsp. yeast extract	1 small leek
1 oz. butter or fat	2–3 celery stalks
1 small carrot	a little salt to taste

Clean the vegetables. Peel the carrot and parsnip. Scrub the celery and leeks. Cut the vegetables in julienne strips (⅛ inch by 1 inch long). Mix the stock (or water) with yeast extract, butter, and salt, and bring to the boil. Add the vegetable strips and boil for about 20 mins. All vegetables should be soft but not broken up.

Broth with Garden Peas (Consommé aux Petits Pois). For 6

2 pt water	1 lb. fresh peas
1 tsp. yeast extract	parsley
1 oz. butter or fat	a little salt to taste

Wash and shell the peas, put the empty pods in 2 pt water and cook for about an hour. Strain and keep the liquid for stock. Allow to cool. Then add the peas, bring to the boil and cook until they are almost tender, add butter or fat, yeast extract, and salt and simmer for another 15 mins. Serve with chopped fresh parsley.

This soup can be made more interesting and nourishing by adding egg balls (page 20) which should be cooked in the soup.

Clear Mushroom Soup. For 6

6–8 oz. mushrooms	¼ lb. French beans
1½ oz. fat or butter	1 tsp. yeast extract
2 carrots	1½ pt stock or water
1 onion	salt to taste
½ stick celery	parsley and/or chives

Wash but do not peel the mushrooms and cut them into thin slices. Put ½ oz. fat in a saucepan, add the sliced mushrooms, and stew for 2 mins. Clean the rest of the vegetables, cut into thin slices, cook in a little stock or water until nearly tender. Now put the rest of the stock (or water) into the soup saucepan together with the cooked vegetables (except the mushrooms), bring to the boil and simmer for about ½ hour. Then add the mushrooms and yeast extract and simmer for another 5 mins. Serve with chopped parsley and/or chives.

This soup should be clear. If you want it more substantial, two large potatoes can be sliced and cooked with the vegetables.

Celery Broth. For 6

2 pt stock or water	1½ oz. butter or fat
2 small or 1 large head of celery	1 tsp. yeast extract
	1 tsp. celery salt or ordinary salt
2 small carrots	parsley

Wash the vegetables, cut the celery into ½-inch pieces, peel and slice the carrots. Melt 1 oz. fat in saucepan, and add the celery. Stew without water for about 5 mins., then add stock or water, celery salt and cook for about ½ hour or until the celery is nearly soft. Add yeast extract, the rest of the fat, and the sliced carrots. Simmer for 10 to 20 mins. until the carrots are soft. Serve with chopped parsley. (The carrots can be left off, or they can be shredded. In both cases the cooking time is reduced.)

Noodle Soup

2 oz. noodles (preferably home-made, page 127)	1½ tsp. yeast extract
	1 oz. fat or butter
2 pt stock or water	salt to taste
chopped parsley	

Boil the stock and fat. Add the noodles and boil until they are soft (15 to 20 mins.). Add yeast extract (if water is used instead of stock use a little more yeast extract), salt, and parsley to taste.

Clear Potato Soup (Soupe Parmentier). For 6

½ lb. potatoes	a few outside cabbage leaves
1½ pt stock or water	1½ oz. butter or fat
2 large carrots	1 tsp. yeast extract
a few sticks of celery	½ tsp. marjoram
1 medium onion	salt to taste

Wash the vegetables, cut the cabbage leaves into narrow strips, peel and cube the rest of the vegetables. Melt 1 oz. fat or butter in a saucepan, add the carrots first (they take longest), then the celery, lastly the cabbage and onion. Stew for about 10 mins. without water on fairly low heat. Stir from time to time to prevent the vegetables from sticking to the saucepan. Add the potatoes and stew another 5 mins. Now, and only now, add ½ pt stock and cook until the vegetables are nearly tender. Add the rest of the stock and fat, and the salt, yeast extract, and marjoram. Cook for another 5 mins. The soup may be slightly cloudy but the vegetables should still be in whole cubes and visible. Serve with croûtons (page 20).

THICK SOUPS

Fresh Tomato Soup. For 4 to 6

1–1½ lb. ripe tomatoes	2 pt stock or
1 large onion	1 pt stock and 1 pt milk or
2 oz. butter or fat	2 pt milk
2 oz. flour	1 small bayleaf
1 Tbs. lemon juice	salt to taste
1 tsp. brown sugar	

Wash the tomatoes and cut them into small pieces. Peel the onion and cut it into small cubes. Melt half the fat in a saucepan and stew the tomatoes together with half the onions until they are soft (no water). Rub the cooked tomatoes and onions through a sieve. Now melt the rest of the fat in a saucepan and add the rest of the onions, cook until golden brown, then add the flour and stew for 3 to 5 mins. Add the sieved tomatoes and the liquid (stock and/or milk) and stew until the flour is well cooked. Add the bayleaf, lemon juice, salt, and sugar. Simmer for another 10 mins. stirring from time to time. This soup is particularly nice when served with grated cheese.

Tomato Soup (made with tomato purée). For 4 to 6

Use the same ingredients and method as in the preceding recipe, but a small tin of tomato purée should be used instead of the fresh tomatoes. Add it after the fat, onions, and flour have been cooked.

Celery Cream Soup. For 4 to 6

2 pt stock, preferably from celery	2 oz. fat or butter
1 large head celery	2 oz. flour
1 tsp. celery salt or ordinary salt	1 tsp. yeast extract
	chopped celery leaves
	1 onion

Wash the celery and cut it into ½-inch strips. Peel and cut the onion into small cubes. Melt ½ oz. fat in a saucepan, add celery, stew for about 5 mins., stirring from time to time. (This is important as it brings out the flavour.) Add ½ pt stock and cook until tender. Melt the rest of the fat in the soup saucepan, add the onions and stew until golden brown. Add the flour and cook for another 2 mins. Then add the rest of the stock and cook for about 5 mins. Add the celery together with the water it was cooked in and cook for another 10 to 20 mins., stirring from time to time. Add yeast extract, celery salt, and chopped celery leaves. Simmer for another 5 mins. and serve.

Some people prefer the celery to be rubbed through a sieve.

A slightly richer soup can be made by substituting milk for half the stock.

Spinach Cream Soup (Potage Florentine). For 4 to 6

1½ lb. spinach	1 pt stock or water
1 large onion	1 pt milk
2 oz. fat	salt and nutmeg to taste
2 oz. flour	

Wash the spinach thoroughly to remove all the earth and grit, and put it in a saucepan. No water need be added as enough usually clings to the spinach from washing. Cook 7 to 10 mins., stirring continuously. Use any water which may then be drained out of the spinach with the stock. Peel the onion and cut it into small cubes. Melt the fat in a saucepan and fry the onions until golden brown, add the flour and cook for about 5 mins., stirring all the time. Add the stock and milk, and cook for another 10 mins. Add the chopped spinach, salt, and very little nutmeg (careful, it may drown the spinach flavour). Serve with croûtons (page 20).

Cauliflower Cream Soup (Crème Dubarry). For 4 to 6

1 large cauliflower	2 oz. flour
1½ pt milk	1 tsp. yeast extract
½ pt stock or water	salt and nutmeg to taste
2 oz. fat or butter	parsley

Cut the cauliflower in small pieces and soak it for about ½ hour in salt water in order to remove any insects. Rinse. Now boil ½ pt milk and the stock or water, add the cauliflower, and cook until soft. Strain and rub the cauliflower through a sieve. Melt the fat in the soup saucepan, add the flour and cook for 5 mins., stirring all the time. Add the rest of the milk and the liquid in which the cauliflower was boiled. Cook for 10 mins. Add the sieved cauliflower, salt, nutmeg, and yeast extract. Simmer for another 5 mins. Serve with chopped parsley.

COOK CAULI, LIQ. ADD MILK & STOCK TO ROUX

Flemish Soup. For 4 to 6

1¼ lb. potatoes	1½ tsp. yeast extract
¼ lb. carrots	2 pt stock or water
2 large onions	1 Tbs. cream or top of milk
1 leek	1 tsp. marjoram
⅓ small head of celery	salt to taste
2 oz. fat or butter	

Wash and peel the vegetables and cut into small pieces, except the onions which should be cut into small cubes. Melt 1½ oz. fat in a saucepan and stew the vegetables without water, starting with the carrots (they take longest), then adding the celery, potatoes, leek, and onions, and stirring from time to time to prevent the vegetables from sticking. This should take about 10 mins. Add 1 pt stock or water and cook until the vegetables are quite soft. Strain and rub vegetables through sieve. Put these and the strained liquid back into a saucepan, add the rest of the stock, or part of it, carefully, keeping the soup fairly thick. Bring to boil and add the rest of the fat, yeast extract, marjoram, and salt, and lastly the cream or top of milk. Simmer for about 20 mins. and serve, preferably with croûtons (page 20).

Bohemian Soup (Vegetable Semolina). For 4 to 6

2 Tbs. semolina	½ small cauliflower
2 pt stock or water	1½ oz. fat or butter
1 small onion	2 tsp. yeast extract
1 leek	1 bayleaf
3 carrots	salt to taste
1 medium turnip	parsley

Clean and peel the vegetables and cut in ½-inch cubes or strips. Melt 1 oz. fat in a saucepan and stew vegetables about 10 mins. (no water), stirring from time to time. Then add stock or water and cook until the vegetables are nearly tender. Add bayleaf. Then pour the dry semolina in, slowly stirring all the time. Cook for another 30 mins., add yeast extract and the last ½ oz. fat. Salt to taste. Serve with chopped parsley.

Vegetable Rice Soup

As previous recipe, but instead of semolina pour 2 Tbs. rice into the boiling soup, and cook for about 20 mins. Particularly tasty if you add 1 tsp. tomato purée or two large tomatoes and a little garlic.

Mixed Vegetable Cream Soup. For 4 to 6

3 carrots	¼ lb. runner beans
1 turnip	any other vegetables, either in
1 parsnip	addition or substitution
1 leek	2½ oz. butter or fat
½ head celery	2 oz. flour
1 medium onion	2 pt stock or water
½ lb. fresh peas	1 bayleaf
(or frozen)	1 tsp. yeast extract

Wash the vegetables, and peel the roots and onions. Cut these into small cubes, the beans into strips. Melt 1 oz. fat in a saucepan, add all the root vegetables and stew for 5 mins., stirring from time to time. Then add the celery, leek, and onion, stew another

2 to 3 mins., add 1 pt stock or water, and cook until tender but not mashy. Boil the peas and beans, if any, separately, until tender. Now mix all vegetables together and strain. Melt the remaining fat in the soup saucepan, add the flour, and stew for a few minutes, stirring all the time. Add the liquid from the strained vegetables and the remaining stock. Cook for about 10 mins. on low heat. Put the vegetables into the boiling mixture, add bayleaf, yeast extract, and salt and simmer for another 10 mins. Serve with chopped parsley.

Cooked vegetables (left-overs, for example) can be used in this soup; they should be added just before the bayleaf and yeast extract. Naturally the quantity of fresh vegetables should be reduced accordingly.

Quick Vegetable Cream Soup (using a liquidizer-blender).
For 2 to 4

1 pt stock or water	few sprigs cauliflower
2 medium potatoes (or one large)	1 oz. butter or fat
	1 medium chopped onion
2 tomatoes	½ tsp. yeast extract
1 carrot	salt to taste
¼ small cabbage	chopped parsley

Wash vegetables and cut in pieces. Put into liquidizer together with the stock or water. Melt fat in a saucepan, add chopped onions, stew until they are light brown. Add liquidized vegetables and cook for 20 mins. Add yeast extract and salt to taste. Serve with chopped parsley.

If cooked (left-over) vegetables (which need not be the same as the named ingredients) are used, the cooking time is only 5 mins.

Fresh Asparagus Soup. For 4 to 6

1 lb. fresh asparagus (use the thin, cheap kind)	2 oz. butter or fat
	2 oz. flour
1 pt water	salt, nutmeg, and parsley to taste
1 pt milk	

Wash the asparagus, cut off the tips and keep them separate.

Cut the rest in pieces about 1 inch long and boil in 1 pt water
for about 30 mins. Strain. The boiled sticks are now tasteless
and can be thrown away. Cook the tips in the asparagus water
for 5 to 10 mins. and strain.

Now melt the fat in a saucepan, add the flour, cook for about
2 mins. over low heat. Mix the asparagus water with the milk
and add a little at a time to the flour and fat mixture, stirring until
all the liquid is absorbed. Simmer for another 5 mins. Add the
asparagus, salt, and nutmeg, heat up once more, and serve with
chopped parsley.

Foreign asparagus has a stronger taste and some people prefer
to use tinned asparagus for that reason; see next recipe.

Asparagus Cream Soup. For 4 to 6

1 medium tin white asparagus	2 oz. fat or butter
1 pt stock or water	2 oz. flour
1 pt milk	salt, nutmeg, and parsley

Open the tin and strain. Use the asparagus water as part of the
stock. Then follow the previous recipe from the second paragraph.

Mushroom Cream Soup. For 4 to 6

½ lb. fresh mushrooms*	2 pt stock or water*
1 large onion	1½ oz. flour
2 oz. fat or butter	yeast extract and salt to taste

Clean and wash the mushrooms. Do not peel them, but cut
them into thin slices. Peel and dice the onion. Melt the fat in a
saucepan, add the onion, and cook for about 5 mins. Add the
sliced mushrooms, cook for another 5 mins. If the mushrooms
are very watery, drain off some of the water which can be used
as part of the stock. Now add the dry flour and cook for another
2 mins. Then the stock or water should be added, little by
little, stirring all the time. Add salt and yeast extract and simmer
for another 10 mins. stirring occasionally. Add chopped parsley
before serving, if desired.

* If water is used instead of stock use more mushrooms.

French Bean Soup (Potage aux Haricots Verts). For 4 to 6

½ lb. French or runner beans	2 oz. flour
2 medium potatoes	½ tsp. yeast extract
1 small onion	½ tsp. savory
2 pt stock or water	salt to taste
2 oz. fat or butter	chopped chives or parsley
2 Tbs. cream or top of milk	

Wash the vegetables. Top and tail the beans, removing the strings. Cut them in ½-inch pieces. Peel the onion and cut it into small cubes. Boil the beans and cubed potatoes in ½ pt of the stock or water until they are soft. Strain, and keep the stock. Fry the onion in the fat (in the soup saucepan) until it is golden brown, add the flour, and stew for about 2 mins. Add the stock and cook until the soup is creamy. Now add the cooked beans and potatoes, the savory, salt, and yeast extract, and cook for another 10 mins. Serve with chopped chives or parsley and add the cream just before serving.

Brown Lentil Soup. For 4 to 6

6 oz. brown lentils	1 pt stock or water
1 large onion	1 pt water
½ lb. potatoes	1 Tbs. lemon juice
2 oz. fat	(or more or less to taste)
1 oz. flour	salt to taste

Wash the lentils, and soak them for at least 12 hours in 1 pt water. Cook them in this water until they are soft. Wash and peel potatoes and onion, cut both into small cubes. Melt 1 oz. fat in a saucepan, add onions and potatoes, and stew for about 5 mins. stirring from time to time. Then add a little stock and cook until the potatoes are soft. Melt the remaining fat in a saucepan, add the flour, and stew for 2 mins. Fill up with the rest of the stock and lentil water and boil for another 5 mins. Then add the lentils, potatoes and onions, salt to taste and the lemon juice. (The lemon juice is a matter of taste and may be left out.) Simmer for another 30 mins.

This is a very thick, substantial soup and can be used as a meal.

Yellow Lentil Soup. For 4 to 6

½ lb. yellow (red) lentils	1 pt stock or water
2 carrots	2 oz. fat
1 leek	1 oz. flour
1 large onion	1 bayleaf
½ lb. potatoes	salt
1 pt water	

While the ingredients of this soup differ slightly from the previous one, the cooking method is exactly the same. Add the cubed carrots and leek with the onion and potatoes.

Yellow Pea Soup. For 4 to 6

½ lb. yellow (dried) peas	2 pt stock or water
¾ lb. potatoes	2 Tbs. cream or top of milk
2 onions	1 tsp. garlic salt or a little
1 carrot	chopped garlic
2 oz. fat	

Wash the peas and soak them for at least 12 hours in 1 pt stock or water. Cook in this stock or water until soft. This may take several hours; if the liquid should get too low add some more. Strain the cooked peas and rub through a sieve. Wash and peel the potatoes, carrots, and onions, and cut them into small pieces. Melt the fat in a saucepan and stew the vegetables for 5 to 10 mins., stirring to prevent them burning. Add the remainder of the stock and boil until all the vegetables are quite soft. Strain and rub the vegetables through a sieve. (If fresh garlic is being used stew it together with the vegetables.) Mix all the vegetables together into the soup, add garlic salt, cook for another 5 mins. and add the cream. Serve with croûtons (page 20).

This soup burns easily, so it is important to keep the heat low and the soup stirred.

Dried green peas can be used instead of the yellow ones; the only difference will be the colour of the soup.

White Bean Soup. For 4 to 6

½ lb. dried haricot beans	1 pt water
1 onion	1 pt stock or water
2 carrots	2 oz. fat
1 leek or stick celery	1 oz. flour
3 medium potatoes	1 tsp. savory
1 bayleaf	salt to taste

Wash the beans and soak them for at least 12 hours in 1 pt water. Cook them in this water until they are quite soft. Melt 1 oz. fat in a saucepan and stew the washed and cubed vegetables for 5 to 10 mins., stirring from time to time. Add the stock or water and cook until tender. Strain the vegetables. Melt the rest of the fat in a saucepan and add the flour. Stew for 2 mins. Then add the stock or bean water, and cook for another 10 mins. Put in all the beans and vegetables; bring to the boil, and cook gently for another 10 mins.

This is a substantial soup and can be served as the main course of a meal. If a very smooth soup is preferred, the vegetables and beans can be rubbed through a sieve before being returned to the creamy soup.

Scotch Broth. For 4 to 6

2 large carrots	2 pt stock or water
1 swede or turnip	2½ oz. butter or fat
2 leeks	1½ tsp. yeast extract
½ head celery	2 oz. pearl barley
2 large onions	salt and nutmeg to taste
2 large potatoes	1 Tbs. cream

Wash the barley and cook separately in 1 pt stock or water until tender. This will take 1 to 1½ hours. Clean and peel the vegetables, and cut them into ½ inch strips or small cubes. Melt 1½ oz. fat in a saucepan and stew the vegetables for 5 to 10 mins., stirring from time to time to prevent sticking. Add 1 pt stock or water, and cook until vegetables are tender. Now mix everything, including the liquid from the barley, together, and add the remaining fat, yeast extract, salt, and nutmeg. Cook gently for another 10 to 15 mins., finally add the cream. Serve with chopped parsley or chives. Can be served as a meal in itself.

COLD FRUIT SOUPS

These are very popular on the Continent during the hot season. We have served them in this country too and have still to meet the person who does not appreciate them. The fruit used should be ripe, in fact it can be slightly over-ripe. Instead of vegetable stock use fruit stock. No fat or milk should ever be added.

Fruit Stock

Most of the fruit for these soups has to be peeled, the plums and cherries stoned, etc. Wash the fruit well. Keep the peel of apples, pears, oranges, and lemons, the cherry stones, etc., for the stock. Add water to cover, to the peel, stones, etc., and cook for about an hour and strain.

Mixed Fruit Soup. For 4 to 6

1 large apple	½ lb. sugar (preferably soft
1 large pear	brown pieces)
1 orange	2 Tbs. cornflour
1 lemon	2 pt fruit stock or water
any other fruit such as	a few ratafia biscuits
strawberries	

Wash and peel the apple, pear, and orange, stone the cherries. Cut the fruit into small pieces, put into fruit stock or water and cook until soft. Squeeze the lemon and add juice to mixture, add the sugar and grated rind of lemon. If the mixture does not taste fruity enough add the juice of another lemon or orange. Bring back to boil. Now mix the cornflour with 2 Tbs. cold water and add this to the boiling soup, stirring all the time. Boil for another 5 mins. and taste. If there is still a pronounced cornflour flavour, boil for a few more minutes. Cool and keep in refrigerator until wanted. Serve with a few ratafia biscuits.

If prepared with a little less water, this can also be used as a sweet.

Cold Apple Soup. For 4 to 6

1 lb. cooking apples	½ lb. sugar
1 large lemon	½ in. cinnamon stick
2 pt fruit stock or water	2 Tbs. semolina

Wash and peel the apples, cut into pieces, and boil in 1 pt water or fruit stock until very soft. Strain and rub through sieve. Add the remaining pint of water or fruit stock. Add the lemon juice, grated rind of lemon, sugar, and cinnamon. Boil for 10 mins., stir in the dry semolina, and cook for about 30 mins. Then take out the cinnamon stick and cool the soup in the refrigerator.

If the soup is to serve as a sweet, use 3 Tbs. semolina instead of two.

Cold Rhubarb Soup. For 4 to 6

1 lb. rhubarb	2 pt water
1 lemon	1 oz. oat flakes
¾ lb. sugar	1 Tbs. vanilla sugar

Wash and brush the rhubarb. Top and tail but do not peel. (The outer skin of rhubarb is edible and gives the soup a nice reddish colour.) Cut in ½-inch pieces and boil in 1 pt water (no fruit stock is needed). When the rhubarb is soft and falls to pieces add the remaining water, sugar, grated rind, lemon juice, and vanilla sugar. Bring to the boil, pour in the oatflakes, and cook gently for 20 to 30 mins. until the oats are soft. Serve ice cold.

Cold Lemon Soup. For 4 to 6

3 lemons	2 Tbs. cornflour
1 orange	1 Tbs. vanilla sugar
2 pt fruit stock or water	2 egg whites
¼ lb. sugar	

Grate the rind of the lemons and orange, and extract the juice from them. Boil the fruit stock or water and sugar for about 10 mins. and add the lemon and orange juice and the grated rind. Mix the cornflour with 2 Tbs. cold water to a smooth cream and pour this into the boiling soup. Cook for another 10 mins. or until the cornflour taste is completely gone. Cool and put into refrigerator. Before serving whip the egg whites together with the vanilla sugar and put a tablespoon of this 'snow' into each plate of soup. Rusks or biscuits can be added as well as, or instead of, the egg snow.

Cold Orange Soup. For 4 to 6

Exactly as previous recipe, but use 6 juicy oranges and only 1 lemon. Ratafia biscuits added to the soup make it look attractive.

Cold Pineapple Soup. For 4 to 6

1 small pineapple	½ lb. sugar
1 lemon	2 pt water
2 in. vanilla pod	2 Tbs. cornflour

Top and tail the pineapple, scrub it carefully, and then peel it. Grate the lemon rind and squeeze the lemon. Now make pineapple stock by boiling the pineapple peel and the otherwise useless remainder of the lemon peel in 1 pt water for half an hour, then strain. Chop the pineapple finely, mix it with 4 oz. sugar, and let it stand for about one hour or longer. Now put the pineapple stock, half the chopped pineapple and the remaining 1 pt water, the grated rind and juice of the lemon, the sugar, and the vanilla pod into a saucepan and cook for 15 mins. Mix the cornflour with 2 Tbs. cold water to a smooth cream and pour into boiling soup. Cook for another 10 mins. Add the remaining chopped pineapple. Serve ice cold.

Cold Strawberry Soup. For 4 to 6

1½ lb. ripe strawberries	1 small lemon
½ lb. sugar	2 pt fruit stock or water
2 Tbs. vanilla sugar	2 Tbs. cornflour

Wash and hull the strawberries. Cut ½ lb. of them (picking the best ones) in halves and mix well with the vanilla sugar. Let them stand for an hour. Boil the remaining strawberries in stock or water for 10 mins., then add the remaining fruit stock or water, the sugar, the grated lemon rind, and the juice. Mix the cornflour with 2 Tbs. cold water to a smooth cream and add to the boiling soup. Cook for another 10 mins., stirring all the time. Take off the flame and add the sugared raw strawberries. Cool and serve ice cold. Can be served with whipped cream.

Cold Raspberry Soup. For 4 to 6

Exactly as previous soup with raspberries instead of strawberries.

Cold Melon Soup. For 4 to 6

1 medium melon	½ lb. sugar
1 lemon	2 Tbs. vanilla sugar
1 orange	2 Tbs. cornflour
2 pt fruit stock or water	½ tsp. ground ginger

Cut the melon in half, take out the pips and pith. (This can be boiled in 2 pt water for 30 mins., then strained and used as fruit stock.) Cut the melon flesh into very small cubes or grate coarsely. Mix this with 2 Tbs. vanilla sugar and let it stand for an hour. Put the fruit stock, sugar, rind, and juice of the orange and lemon into the saucepan and boil for 5 mins. Mix the cornflour with 2 Tbs. water to a cream and pour into the boiling soup. Cook for another 10 mins., stirring all the time. Add sugared melon and ginger. Cool.

To make the soup more interesting mix 1 tsp. of raspberry syrup into the centre of each plate before serving.

Cold Cherry Soup. For 4 to 6

1½ lb. cooking cherries (morello)	2 Tbs. cornflour
1 lemon	¼ pt whipped cream
2 pt fruit stock or water	½ in. cinnamon stick or
12 oz. sugar	¼ tsp. ground cinnamon

Wash and stone the cherries. Cook them in the fruit stock or water with the cinnamon for about 10 mins., then add the sugar and grated rind and juice of the lemon. Remove the cinnamon stick. Mix the cornflour in 2 Tbs. cold water and pour into the boiling soup. Cook for another 10 mins., stirring all the time. Cool and serve with a spoonful of whipped cream.

Cold Plum Soup. For 4 to 6

1½ lb. ripe plums	2 Tbs. cornflour
¼ lb. sugar	½ in. cinnamon stick or
1 lemon	¼ tsp. ground cinnamon
2 pt fruit stock or water	

Cooking method as previous recipe.

UNUSUAL SOUPS

Every one of these unusual recipes has its own specific character – and its group of addicts. For those who have the time and inclination to experiment a little they provide a challenge and the opportunity to produce something extra exciting for the family or party.

Minestrone (Thick Italian Vegetable Soup). For 6. A meal in itself.

2 oz. haricot beans	½ lb. fresh tomatoes or
2 oz. spaghetti	small tin of purée
2 small carrots	2 oz. butter or fat
¼ stick celery	2 oz. grated cheese
1 medium onion	2 pt vegetable stock or water
2 small potatoes	chopped parsley, marjoram,
(or one large)	chives, garlic to taste
1 bayleaf	½ tsp. yeast extract

Wash the beans and soak them for at least 12 hours. Cook them in the same water until soft (this may take up to two hours). Cook the spaghetti in about 1 pt salt water until soft (about 15 mins.).

In the meantime wash and peel the vegetables and cut them into small cubes. Melt the fat in a saucepan and add: first the carrots (they take longest); a little later the celery; then the onions; and lastly the potatoes. Stew for about 10 mins. stirring from time to time to prevent sticking. Then add the cut tomatoes (but not the purée if that is what you are using), and only now add about half the water or stock. Cook until all the vegetables are tender. The cooked beans and spaghetti together with the water they were cooked in (if it does not make too much liquid) should be added, as well as the remaining stock, yeast extract, salt, bayleaf, and marjoram, and the finely chopped garlic if desired. Bring to the boil and simmer for at least another half hour. (The flavour will improve with simmering.) If tomato purée is used, add it just before the soup is done.

Serve with a good helping of grated cheese and a little chopped chives and parsley in each plate.

Mulligatawny (Curried Vegetable Soup). For 4 to 6

2 medium carrots	2 pt stock or water
1 leek	2½ oz. fat
1 stick celery	2 tsp. curry powder
1 medium turnip or swede	½ oz. sultanas
1 small cooking apple	1 bayleaf
2 small onions	1–1½ oz. flour
1 oz. cooked white beans	lemon juice and salt to taste

Clean and cube the vegetables. Peel one onion and cut it into small cubes. Melt 1 oz. fat in saucepan and stew the vegetables (without water) for 5 to 10 mins., stirring from time to time. Add 1 pt stock or water and cook until all vegetables are tender. Add the cooked beans. Melt the remaining fat in the soup saucepan, add the other onion and the apple, finely chopped, together with the washed sultanas, and stew for about 5 mins. Add the flour and stew for another 2 mins., stirring all the time. Add the curry powder, salt, and bayleaf, and stew for another 2 mins. Pour in the remaining stock, and cook and stir for 5 mins. after the soup has become creamy. Now all the cooked vegetables are added and another 10 mins. later the soup will be well blended. Lastly, add the lemon juice.

If a stronger curry taste is required, increase the amount of curry powder.

Cheese Soup. For 4 to 6

3 oz. Cheddar or Parmesan cheese, grated	½ pt milk
2 oz. flour	2–3 Tbs. cream
3 oz. butter or fat	1 tsp. yeast extract
1½ pt stock or water	salt and nutmeg to taste
	chopped parsley

Melt 2½ oz. fat in a saucepan, stir in the flour and stew for about 2 mins. Add the milk and stock or water and cook for 15 to 20 mins., stirring from time to time to prevent burning. Add the yeast extract, salt, nutmeg, and the remaining ½ oz. of fat. Take the soup off the flame, and add the cheese only after the soup has stopped bubbling (otherwise the cheese will get rubbery). Stir to dissolve the cheese and serve with chopped parsley.

Bortsch (Russian Beetroot Soup). For 4 to 6

3 medium raw beetroots	2 pt stock or water
2 carrots	¼ pt sour cream
1 onion	2 Tbs. lemon juice or
½ small cabbage	vinegar
2 leeks	2 tsp. sugar
2 oz. fat (no butter)	1 bayleaf and salt to taste

Clean and peel the vegetables, and cut them into small strips or cubes, except for one beetroot. Melt 1 oz. fat in a saucepan and stew in it the cut beetroots for a few minutes, then add the rest of the cut vegetables and stew for another 5 to 10 mins., stirring from time to time. Add the stock (or water) and cook until the vegetables are tender. Add the bayleaf, lemon juice (or vinegar), sugar, and salt, and cook for another 10 mins. Now grate the remaining beetroot into the soup, or, if preferred, squeeze the grated beetroot through a muslin cloth and add the juice only. Top with the sour cream just before serving.

Salsify Soup. For 4 to 6

1 lb. salsify	½ tsp. yeast extract
2 medium onions	½ lemon
2 oz. fat or butter	salt and nutmeg to taste
2 oz. flour	chopped parsley
1½ pt stock or water	2 egg yolks
1 pt milk	

Salsify, after being washed and peeled, easily turns black. So peel it under running water, and cut it quickly into 1-inch pieces which should go immediately into a saucepan filled with 1 pt stock or water with a few drops of lemon juice. Cook until the salsify is soft. While it is boiling, melt the fat in a saucepan, add the cubed onions, and stew until light brown. Mix in the flour, stew for another 2 mins., add the liquid from the salsify and the milk, and cook for about 10 mins., stirring until the soup is creamy. Then add the cooked salsify and the grated lemon rind, yeast extract, salt, and nutmeg to taste. Let the soup cool off a little. Add the lemon juice very slowly and stir to prevent the soup from curdling.

The following method of adding egg yolks makes the soup richer and very smooth (the chefs call it *velouté* = velvety). Beat the egg yolks in a small mixing or pudding bowl and add 1 Tbs. of warm (not boiling) soup very gradually, beat and add another Tbs. and so on until the bowl is full. Then pour this mixture back into the soup and serve. On no account must the soup be boiled up again.

Camélia Soup (Peas and Rice). For 4 to 6

6 oz. split peas	2½ pt stock or water
½ lb. potatoes	1 clove garlic or
1 large onion	½ tsp. garlic salt
1 leek	salt to taste
2 oz. rice	2 egg yolks
2 oz. fat or butter	

Wash, soak, and cook the peas as for Yellow Pea Soup (page 30). Peel the potatoes, cut them into large cubes, and boil them in stock or water until very soft. Strain the peas and rub them through a sieve. Mix with the potatoes, add 1 oz. fat, and mash. Peel and cut the onions and garlic into very small cubes, and the leek into strips. Now melt the remaining 1 oz. fat in a saucepan, add the onions, garlic, and leeks, stew for 3 to 5 mins., and then add the washed rice. Stir and watch that the rice does not turn brown. After another 3 mins. (or earlier if the rice shows signs of turning brown) add the stock and pea water and cook until the rice is soft. Mix together with the mashed potatoes and peas, season with salt and/or garlic salt, bring to the boil again, and simmer for another 10 to 15 mins. Enrich with egg yolks as previous recipe.

Potage Solférino

This is a mixture of Tomato Soup (page 23) and Flemish Soup (page 25), half and half, enriched with egg yolks as in Salsify Soup (page 38).

Rich Asparagus Cream Soup

Asparagus Soup (page 27) enriched with egg yolks.

Potage Carmen

Tomato Soup (page 23) with added cooked rice and strips of green pepper.

Potage d'Oignons des Viveurs (French Onion Soup with Cheese Toasties)

¾ lb. onions	1 pt stock or water
3 oz. fat	2 peppercorns
1½ oz. flour	1 bayleaf
1 pt milk	salt to taste

Peel the onions and cut them into thick slices. Boil about three quarters of the onions in the milk together with the bayleaf and peppercorns until the onions are quite soft. Strain (keeping the liquid separate), and remove the bayleaf and peppercorns. Stew the remaining raw onions in 1 oz. fat until they are soft but still white. If the onions should start getting yellow add some stock or water quickly. Then rub the cooked and fried onions through a sieve.

Melt the remaining 2 oz. fat in a saucepan, add the flour, and stew for 2 mins., stirring all the time. Then add the milk the onions were cooked in and the stock (or water) and cook for 5 to 7 mins., stirring continuously. Finally add the sieved onions.

Cheese Toasties

1½ oz. cheese	1 tsp. French mustard
2 Tbs. flour	4 slices of toast
¾ cup milk	a few grains cayenne pepper
1 oz. butter	a little salt to taste

Melt the butter in a small saucepan, add the flour, and stew for
1 or 2 mins., add the milk and stew for another 2 to 3 mins.
Take off the flame and add half the grated cheese, mustard, salt,
and cayenne pepper. Mix well together and spread this mixture
on the toast. Top with the remaining grated cheese and put
under hot grill until the top is golden brown. Cut into ½-inch
squares.

Add these toasties to the soup at the last minute (or serve
separately) so that they do not get soggy.

Vegetables

Vegetables contain important vitamins and minerals and form a vital part in any health-giving diet. Gradually we are getting away from the idea that they are mere garnishes or decorations, an idea which formerly held good in commercial kitchens where the vegetable cook occupied the lowliest position, and was required only to clean the vegetables, put them in a large pot with plenty of water, and cook them slowly to death. Too much water prolongs the cooking process unnecessarily and not only kills the vitamins but also leaches out other nutritive elements. Most vegetables need only a very short cooking time, as you will see from the times given in these recipes; allowance should, incidentally, be made for variations in freshness. It is never necessary or desirable to add bicarbonate of soda.

Boiling (steaming) is perhaps not the most exciting way of cooking vegetables, but for low-calorie and slimming diets it plays an important part. Very little water should be used; in most cases, it will have disappeared when the vegetables are ready. (The saucepan lid should always be on.) Alternatively a steamer can be used, that is a saucepan with a strainer inserted, so that the vegetables do not come in contact with the water. The cooking time for steaming is longer, but can be reduced by using a pressure cooker.

The best method, in our view, is sometimes called 'conservative' cooking. It is the same basic method as used for delicious Chinese vegetable cooking. A little fat is melted in a saucepan, the vegetables added and stewed for about 5 mins., then a little stock or water is added and they are stewed for another 5 to 10 mins. This is also the quickest way, and it combines the advantages of both frying and boiling without the disadvantage both these methods entail. It also preserves nearly all the goodness.

If a slightly more substantial end product is required, this method can be modified by adding milk, cream, flour, or other ingredients to make it a 'creamed' or *à la crème* vegetable.

There are, besides, other tasty ways of preparing vegetables which will be dealt with under appropriate headings.

Freshness is of course an important quality. Home-grown vegetables straight from the garden are the best to use, particularly if in addition they have been grown without chemical fertilizers and sprays. (Such 'compost-grown' vegetables are occasionally obtainable in health-food stores.) However, with today's fast air transport fresh vegetables are available all the year round, and frozen ones are usually very good too; we prefer them to tinned ones, as the quality is usually better and no preservative, or very little, is added.

SIMPLE VEGETABLE DISHES

Steamed Jerusalem Artichokes. For 4

1½ lb. artichokes	water, with salt to taste
1½ oz. fat or butter	chopped parsley

Scrub the artichokes carefully, peel them very thinly and keep them until you are ready to use them in water in which 1 Tbs. flour and 2 Tbs. vinegar have been dissolved. (This will prevent them becoming discoloured.) Cut the artichokes in thick slices or quarter them, put them into a saucepan with just enough water to cover them, and boil until soft but not mashy. Strain. Melt the fat in a saucepan, add the strained artichokes and parsley, heating up while shaking the saucepan to prevent sticking.

Baked Jerusalem Artichokes. For 4

1½ lb. artichokes	1 tsp. salt
1 Tbs. oil	

Scrub the artichokes carefully. Oil a baking sheet. Cut the large artichokes in halves; the small ones can be left whole. Brush each artichoke with a little oil, sprinkle a very small pinch of salt on each, and put them on the baking sheet. Bake in a hot

oven (400°, Reg. 6) for about ¾ to one hour. The skin will be
tender and can be eaten but some people prefer it removed.

Creamed Jerusalem Artichokes. For 4

1½ lb. artichokes	½ pt milk or stock or water
1 oz. fat	juice of ½ lemon
1 oz. flour	salt and nutmeg to taste

Cook the artichokes as for Steamed Jerusalem Artichokes. Melt
the fat in a saucepan, add the flour, stew for about 5 mins.,
stirring all the time. Add the milk and the stock or artichoke
water (or a mixture of these), and cook for another 5 mins. Add
salt, nutmeg, and lemon juice, then the strained artichokes and
heat up again, stirring carefully.

Jerusalem Artichokes Sauté. For 4

1½ lb. artichokes	salt to taste
2–3 Tbs. oil	

Scrub or peel the artichokes, cover them with water, and boil
until they are about half cooked. Strain, cut them into cubes or
thin slices. Heat the oil in a frying pan, add the artichokes and
salt, fry until golden brown.

Jerusalem Artichokes with Tomato Sauce. For 4

1½ lb. artichokes
½ pt Tomato Sauce (page 101)

Cook artichokes as in Steamed Jerusalem Artichokes. Make
Tomato Sauce and mix together.

Jerusalem Artichokes Béchamel (with Onion). For 4

1½ lb. artichokes	1 oz. fat
1 medium onion	1 oz. flour
1 Tbs. lemon juice	nutmeg and salt to taste
½ pt stock or water	chopped parsley
½ pt milk or water	

Cook the artichokes as in Steamed Jerusalem Artichokes and
strain. Peel and chop the onion finely. Fry it in ½ oz. fat until

soft but not brown. Melt the rest of the fat in a saucepan, add the fried onions and the flour, stew for 2 mins. Add the milk, stock or artichoke water (or a mixture of these) and cook for 5 mins., stirring all the time. Lastly add the nutmeg, salt, and lemon juice. Put in the strained artichokes, heat up, and serve with chopped parsley.

Jerusalem Artichokes with Sauce Hollandaise

Cook the artichokes as in Steamed Jerusalem Artichokes. Make a Sauce Hollandaise (page 98) and serve it separately.

Jerusalem Artichokes au Gratin (1). For 4

1½ lb. artichokes	Cheese Sauce (page 97)
1 oz. grated cheese	½ oz. fat or butter

Cook artichokes as for Steamed Jerusalem Artichokes. Strain. (The water can be used to make the cheese sauce.) Put them in a buttered fireproof dish. Pour on the cheese sauce and sprinkle the grated cheese on top. Bake in a moderate oven (350°, Reg. 4) for 30 to 35 mins.

Jerusalem Artichokes au Gratin (2). For 4

1½ lb. artichokes	3 Tbs. stock or water
1 oz. fat or butter	2 oz. grated cheese
2 Tbs. cream	salt to taste

Cook artichokes as for Steamed Jerusalem Artichokes. Strain and keep hot. Butter a fireproof dish with ½ oz. butter (or fat). Add the stock (or water), the artichokes, the grated cheese, the cream, and finally the rest of the butter (or fat) cut into small pieces on top. Bake in hot oven (400°, Reg. 7) for 30 mins.

Asparagus

Allow 5 to 8 sticks per person. Scrub the white ends, which are usually dirty. Trim off a little of the bottom end, then scrape or peel the white part. Do not touch the heads as they break off easily, particularly after cooking. Make a bundle of each portion by tying cotton round the white ends. Boil until tender, about

30 mins., in enough water to cover the bundles but, if possible, not the heads. This can easily be done in a tall pan in which the asparagus can stand upright or in a special asparagus cooker. Take the bundles out carefully, put on the serving plate and remove the cotton.

Serve with: hot (browned) butter; Sauce Hollandaise (page 98); Sauce Mousseline (page 100); or cold with Vinaigrette (page 171).

NOTE. The asparagus water, the peel, and the trimmed off ends are excellent for stock and asparagus soup.

Broad Beans. For 4

2 lb. young broad beans or 3–4 lb. if old	2 Tbs. fat or butter chopped parsley

If the beans are very young prepare like Runner Beans (page 47) but slice across. If they are fairly young, take out the beans and slice the good green parts of the pods. Otherwise use only the beans. Cook the beans, together with the pods if used, in enough water to cover them, for about 20 to 25 mins. Strain, melt the butter in a saucepan, add the beans, toss and serve with chopped parsley.

Broad Beans Béchamel (with Onion). For 4

2 lb. young broad beans or 3–4 lb. old ones	1 pt milk or stock or water
1 medium onion	1 tsp. yeast extract
2 oz. fat or butter	¼ tsp. dried savory or fresh sprigs
2 oz. flour	salt to taste

Cook the beans as in the previous recipe. Strain. Melt the fat in a saucepan, add the peeled and finely cut onion, and stew until golden brown. Add the flour and stew for another 3 to 5 mins., stirring all the time, then add the milk and stock or bean water and cook for about 10 mins. Add the savory, yeast extract and salt, then the beans, and heat up again.

Creamed Broad Beans. For 4

As previous recipe but leave out the onion.

Runner Beans. For 4

2 lb. beans
2 Tbs. fat or butter
salt to taste

chopped parsley
a little savory, fresh or dried

Wash and top and tail the beans. Break or cut into 2-inch pieces, or – better – slice lengthwise. Cook in just enough water to cover the beans, about 10 to 20 mins. Strain. Melt the butter in a saucepan, add the beans, savory, and parsley, and heat up, stirring gently.

French Beans (Haricots Verts). For 4

These may be cooked in the same way as the previous recipe but the beans will cook more quickly, in 7 to 15 mins.

NOTE. Runner beans and French beans can be cooked creamed and Béchamel in the same way as broad beans.

French Beans and Carrots à la Crème. For 4

1 lb. French beans
1 lb. carrots

$\frac{1}{2}$–1 pt Cream Sauce (page 95)

Cook the beans as in the previous recipe and strain. Wash and peel the carrots and cut them into thin slices. Use a little of the bean water and cook the carrots until tender, not longer than 10 mins. Strain if there is any water left. Make a cream sauce, put in the vegetables, and heat up again.

Runner Beans and White (Dried) Beans. For 4

1 lb. runner beans
$\frac{1}{2}$ lb. white (dried) beans

Cream Sauce (page 95)

Wash the white beans and soak them for at least 12 hours. Cook them in the water they have soaked in for 1 to 1$\frac{1}{2}$ hours or until they are soft but still whole. Cook the runner beans as above Strain both kinds of beans and use the bean water for cream sauce. Put the beans back into the sauce, heat up, and serve.

This is a very substantial vegetable dish. Left-over beans of either kind can be used.

Cooked Beetroots

Most greengrocers sell beetroots ready-cooked. However, here is the way to cook them. Allow 6 oz. per person. Scrub them carefully to remove the soil but try not to break the skin or the lovely red juice will leak out and be lost. Cut off the leaves but leave the tap root on. Cook in water until soft. The time depends entirely on how old the beetroots are. They are done if the skin comes off easily when the beetroots are pressed between finger and thumb. Young beetroots will need little more than ½ hour; as they get older they may take up to 2 hours.

Creamed Beetroots. For 4

1½ lb. cooked beetroots	1 Tbs. sugar
1 oz. butter or fat	2 Tbs. vinegar or lemon juice
1 oz. flour	salt to taste
½ bayleaf	

Skin and cut the beetroots into cubes. Melt the fat in a saucepan, add the flour, stir, and stew for 2 mins. Mix the vinegar or lemon juice with ½ pt water, add this mixture and cook for another 5 mins., stirring all the time. Add the bayleaf, sugar, and salt, then the beetroots, and cook slowly for another 5 mins.

Broccoli

Young broccoli can be used alone as a vegetable in the same way as spring greens, or – better – in Creamed Mixed Greens (page 59). But this vegetable is normally eaten when it is older and purple sprigs have formed which resemble, and are cooked in the same way as, cauliflower. They taste best if cooked like Stewed Cauliflower (page 54).

Steamed Brussels Sprouts. For 4

2 lb. sprouts

Trim the outer leaves and cut a cross into the stem at the bottom. (This allows the heat to penetrate more quickly and shortens the cooking time.) Wash the sprouts thoroughly in salt water; it is a good idea to leave them in this water for about 15 mins. to get any insects out. There is usually enough water clinging to the sprouts for them to start cooking without any more water being added. If they do run dry, add a very little water. Do not add bicarbonate of soda.

This may sound more complicated than the old-fashioned way of cooking them in plenty of water but the cooking time is very much shortened (5 to 7 mins.) and the result is most rewarding.

Stewed Brussels Sprouts. For 4

2 lb. sprouts
1½ oz. fat (not butter)

Wash the sprouts as in the previous recipe. Melt the fat in a saucepan, and when it is hot add the sprouts without any water. Cook for 5 to 7 mins. If the sprouts start sticking, add a little (very little) water. Add salt, if desired, just before serving.

This is the best way of cooking sprouts although they may lose a little of their green colour.

Creamed Brussels Sprouts. For 4

2 lb. sprouts
1 oz. fat (not butter)
1 oz. flour
½ pt milk or stock or water
salt and nutmeg to taste
chopped parsley

Cook sprouts as for steamed. Strain if necessary. Melt the fat in a saucepan, add the flour, and stew for 2 mins. Add the milk, stock, or water, salt, and nutmeg and cook over a low heat for 5 to 10 mins. Add the sprouts and heat up gently. Serve with chopped parsley.

Brussels Sprouts au Gratin. For 4

2 lb. sprouts
1 oz. grated cheese
Cheese Sauce (page 97)
½ oz. fat

Cook sprouts as for steamed. Grease a fireproof dish with fat (no butter), put in the cooked sprouts and the cheese sauce, sprinkle the grated cheese on top, and bake in moderate oven (350°, Reg. 4) for 40 mins.

Brussels Sprouts with Carrots à la Crème. For 4

1½ lb. sprouts
½ lb. carrots
Cream Sauce (page 95)
salt to taste

Cook sprouts as for steamed. Peel the carrots, cut them into slices, cook them for 10 mins. in very little water, and strain. Make the cream sauce using, if you wish, the carrot water, mix in the strained carrots and a little later the sprouts, and serve as soon as the vegetables are hot.

Brussels Sprouts with Chestnuts. For 4

1½ lb. sprouts   chestnuts cooked as in next
1 oz. fat   recipe

Cook sprouts as for stewed. Serve on a large plate, the chestnuts in the centre, the sprouts placed around them.

Chestnuts. For 4 as addition to another vegetable

1 lb. chestnuts   ½ pt milk or stock
1 small onion   1 tsp. sugar
1 oz. fat   a little salt

Wash the chestnuts (the edible kind of course) and cut a cross in the skins. Boil until the cross opens. Then try one and see whether the peel and brown skin can be peeled off (the chestnut itself need not be soft); if not, boil a little longer. Then peel all the chestnuts and cut them in halves. Melt the fat in a saucepan and stew the peeled and finely chopped onion for 2 mins., then add the chestnuts and stew for 5 to 7 mins., stirring from time to time. Now add the milk or stock, salt, and sugar and cook over a low heat until all the liquid has disappeared. The chestnuts should now be soft but not mashy.

Steamed Green Cabbage. For 4

2 lb. cabbage
½ cup stock or water

Cut cabbage in quarters. Wash in salt water, drain, and shred coarsely. Wash again and put in a saucepan with washing water still clinging to the cabbage. Boil for 5 to 7 mins. adding a little water only if the cabbage starts sticking. Do not use bicarbonate of soda. Serve at once.

Here again the taste and food value are much better than when using the old method of cooking cabbage in lots of water.

Stewed Green Cabbage. For 4

2 lb. cabbage	1 oz. fat (not butter)
1 small onion	salt to taste

Clean and shred cabbage as in previous recipe. Melt the fat in a saucepan and add the peeled and finely chopped onion. Stew for 2 mins., then add the wet, shredded cabbage and stew for 5 to 7 mins., shaking the saucepan or stirring gently with a wooden spoon from time to time to prevent sticking. Serve at once.

Green Cabbage in Tomato Sauce. For 4

2 lb. cabbage
Tomato Sauce (page 101)

Cook cabbage as for steamed. Make tomato sauce and mix before serving.

Red Cabbage (Bavarian Style). For 4

1½ lb. red cabbage	4 cloves
1 small onion	1 bayleaf
2 Tbs. lemon juice or vinegar	1 large apple
1½ oz. fat (not butter)	1 Tbs. sugar
1 tsp. cornflour	½ in. cinnamon stick
½ pt stock or water	

Cut the cabbage in quarters and wash it. Shred finely and wash again. Melt the fat in a saucepan, add the cabbage and stew for 3 to 4 mins., shaking the saucepan to prevent sticking. Add the whole peeled onion into which the cloves have been stuck, then the bayleaf, lemon juice or vinegar, sugar, and cinnamon. Stew for another 10 mins. Then add the stock or water. Wash the apple and cut it into large cubes – the skin and core can be left on – add them to the pan, and cook for another 30 to 35 mins. The apple should by now be quite soft and have practically disappeared into the cabbage. Now remove the cinnamon stick, the onion with cloves, and the bayleaf. Dissolve the cornflour in a little cold water and add to the cabbage. Cook for another 2 to 3 mins.

This typically Bavarian dish goes specially well with Apple Fritters (page 134) or Baked Potatoes (page 104) or both.

Red Cabbage with Chestnuts. For 4

Red Cabbage (previous recipe)
Chestnuts (page 50)

Either mix both together before serving, or serve cabbage on large plate with the chestnuts around.

Stewed White Cabbage with Caraway. For 4

1½ lb. white cabbage   ½ pt stock or water
1 small onion   1½ oz. fat (not butter)
½ tsp. caraway seeds   salt to taste

Cut the cabbage in quarters and wash it. Shred finely and wash again. Strain. Melt the fat in a saucepan, add the peeled and chopped onion, stew for 2 mins., add the cabbage, and stew for another 5 to 10 mins., shaking the saucepan from time to time. Then add the stock or water and cook for another 15 mins. Add salt and caraway seeds, heat up again, and serve.

Steamed Carrots. For 4

2 lb. carrots   chopped parsley or chives
½ cup water or stock   a little sugar
salt to taste

Wash and peel the carrots; if they are very young they can be cooked whole, otherwise slice or cube them. Bring the stock or water to the boil, add the carrots, cook for about 10 mins. add salt and sugar to tast. Serve with chopped parsley and/or chives.

Stewed Carrots. For 4

2 lb. carrots   2 Tbs. water or stock
1 oz. fat or butter   chopped parsley

Wash and peel the carrots and cut them into thin slices. Melt the fat in a saucepan, add the carrots, and stew for 2 mins., shaking the saucepan from time to time. Add the stock or water and stew for another 5 mins. Serve with chopped parsley.

Creamed Carrots. For 4

2 lb. carrots	½ pt milk, water, or stock
1½ oz. butter or fat	½ tsp. yeast extract
1½ oz. flour	½ tsp. sugar
salt to taste	

Wash and peel the carrots, and cut them into cubes. Bring ½ cup of water to the boil and cook the carrots for about 10 mins. If the water has not evaporated, strain. Now melt the fat in a saucepan, add the flour, stew for 2 mins., then add the milk, stock, or water and cook for another 5 mins., stirring all the time. Add the carrots, sugar, salt, and yeast extract and heat up again. Serve at once.

Mashed Carrots. For 4

1½ lb. carrots	1½ oz. fat or butter
½ lb. potatoes	chopped parsley
1 small onion	salt to taste

Wash and peel the carrots, cut them into large cubes and cook in a little water (just covering the carrots) until quite soft. Strain and mash. Do the same with the potatoes separately. Now mix the two vegetables together in a saucepan, add ½ cup of the carrot water, 1 oz. fat or butter, and salt to taste. Heat up, and while doing so beat with a strong whisk to prevent the mixture from sticking and to make it light and somewhat fluffy. Meanwhile fry the finely cubed onion in the rest of the fat until golden brown; then pour both fat and onions over the finished vegetables and sprinkle with the chopped parsley.

Carrots Vichy. For 4

2 lb. carrots	1 tsp. sugar
1–1½ Tbs. chopped parsley	salt to taste
2 oz. fat or butter	

Wash and peel the carrots, cut into thin slices. Melt the fat in a saucepan, add carrots, sugar, and salt. Stew slowly until the carrots are soft. Do not add water, but stir gently all the time. Before serving add the parsley (the full amount is important for this dish) and toss the carrots in it.

Carrots and Celery à la Crème. For 4

1 lb. carrots	Cream Sauce (page 95)
1 medium head celery	yeast extract

Cook carrots as for steamed. Celery as on page 55. Make cream sauce and mix all three together. Add yeast extract to taste.

Carrots and Peas à la Crème. For 4

1 lb. carrots	Cream Sauce (page 95)
1½ lb. peas or	yeast extract
small packet frozen peas	salt to taste

Cook carrots as for steamed. Peas as on page 66. Make cream sauce. Mix all three together. Add yeast extract and salt to taste.

NOTE. Carrots and peas are a particularly tasty combination.

Carrots au Gratin. For 4

2 lb. carrots	Cheese Sauce (page 97)
½ oz. fat or butter	1 oz. grated cheese

Cook carrots as for steamed, make cheese sauce, and mix the two. Put the mixture into a buttered fireproof dish and sprinkle the grated cheese on top. Bake for 40 mins. in a moderate oven (350°, Reg. 4–5).

Steamed Cauliflower. For 4

1 large cauliflower
1 cup of water

Remove the outside leaves (they can be used for Vegetable Stock, or Mixed Greens, page 59) and separate the sprigs. The tender inside leaves and stalk can be used. Wash the cauliflower in salt water, leaving it for 20 mins. in the water. Strain and wash again under running water to remove any insects that are left. Bring the cup of water to the boil in a saucepan, add the cauliflower and cook for 7 to 10 mins., then add the salt. Strain and serve.

Stewed Cauliflower. For 4

1 large cauliflower
2 oz. fat (not butter)

Wash and prepare the cauliflower as in previous recipe. Melt the fat in a saucepan, add the cauliflower and stew for 5 to 7 mins., shaking the saucepan to prevent sticking. If the cauliflower shows signs of browning, add a little water. Salt to taste.

Cauliflower au Gratin. For 4

1 large cauliflower	½ oz. fat (not butter)
Cheese Sauce (page 97)	1 oz. grated cheese

Cook the cauliflower as for steamed. Make cheese sauce. Grease a fireproof dish with fat (not butter), put the cauliflower and cheese sauce in it, with the grated cheese sprinkled on top. Bake in a moderate oven (350°, Reg. 4–5) for 30 mins.

Cauliflower in Tomato Sauce. For 4

Cook the cauliflower as for steamed. Make Tomato Sauce (page 101). Mix.

Cauliflower with Sauce Hollandaise. For 4

Cook the cauliflower as for steamed. Make Sauce Hollandaise (page 99). Serve the two separately.

Fried Cauliflower Polonaise. For 4

1 cooked cauliflower	breadcrumbs
1 large egg	oil for deep frying
2 Tbs. milk	salt to taste

Divide the cauliflower into large sprigs and dry in a towel. Leftovers can be used. Beat the egg and milk together, adding salt if desired, dip the cauliflower sprigs into this mixture and cover them with breadcrumbs. Fry in deep fat (oil) until golden brown.

Steamed Celery. For 4

2 medium heads celery
1 cup water or stock

Clean and brush celery thoroughly, then rinse it under running water. The outside stems, if properly cleaned, and the young green leaves can be left on and used. Cut into 2-inch pieces and cook until tender, about 20 mins.

Stewed Celery. For 4

2 medium heads celery	⅓ cup water or stock
1 oz. fat or butter	½ tsp. yeast extract

Clean and cut the celery up as in the previous recipe. Melt the fat in a saucepan, add the celery and stew for about 5 mins., shaking the saucepan from time to time. Add the stock or water and cook for another 5 to 10 mins.; by then most of the water should have been absorbed. Add the yeast extract and serve.

Creamed Celery. For 4

2 medium heads celery	½ cup milk
1½ oz. fat or butter	½ tsp. yeast extract
1½ oz. flour	a little salt or celery salt

Cook the celery as for steamed. Melt the fat in a saucepan, add the flour, and stew for 2 mins., stirring all the time. Add 1 cup of the celery water, the milk, and the salt, and cook for 3 to 5 mins., stirring again. Put strained celery into the mixture, add the yeast extract, and heat up again.

Celery au Gratin. For 4

2 medium heads celery	Cheese Sauce (page 97)
1 oz. fat or butter	1 oz. grated cheese

Cook the celery as for steamed. Strain and mix with cheese sauce. Butter a fireproof dish and put in the mixture. Sprinkle grated cheese on top and bake for 30 mins. in a hot oven (400°, Reg. 6–7).

Braised Celery. For 4

2 medium heads celery	1½ tsp. yeast extract
2 oz. butter or fat	1 bayleaf
1 Tbs. cornflour	2 peppercorns
½ pt stock or water	salt to taste

Wash and cut the celery up as for steamed. Melt 1 oz. fat in a casserole and put the pieces of celery in it. Add less than half the stock or water, cover, and cook in moderate oven (350°, Reg. 4–5) for about 30 mins. The celery should be nearly soft.

In the meantime make a sauce by boiling the rest of the stock or celery water with the bayleaf, peppercorns, and the rest of the fat for about 10 mins. Then take out the bayleaf and peppercorns, and add yeast extract and salt. Mix the cornflour with 2 Tbs. cold water and add to the boiling sauce, cook for 5 mins., stirring all the time. Now pour the sauce over the celery in the casserole dish and leave in the oven for another 10 to 15 mins.

Celery and Garden Peas à la Crème. For 4

1 head celery
Cream Sauce (page 95)

1½ lb. peas or small packet
of frozen peas

Cook the celery as for steamed and the peas separately as on page 66. Make cream sauce, mix all together, and serve.

Celery and Tomatoes. For 4

1 head celery
1 lb. tomatoes

1½ oz. fat or butter
1 small onion

Stew the celery with half the fat. Wash the tomatoes and cut them in halves. Peel and cube the onion. Melt the rest of the fat in a saucepan and fry the onion golden brown. Add the tomatoes and stew for a few mins.; they should not get mashy. Add the stewed celery carefully, and a little pinch of salt, if desired. This dish can also be served with grated cheese.

Boiled Chicory. For 4

1 lb. chicory
½ lemon

Remove the outside leaves if they are brown and trim off the brown part of the stem. Cut in half and wash carefully. Bring 1 pt water to the boil, squeeze in the juice of half a lemon. Add the chicory and cook for 10 to 15 mins. Drain and serve with a very little chopped parsley, if desired.

NOTE. The lemon juice not only gives the chicory a delicate flavour but will also keep it white. The chicory water is bitter and cannot be used for anything.

Chicory with Marmite Sauce. For 4

1 lb. chicory	⅓ pt stock or water
1½ oz. butter or fat	2 tsp. Marmite
1½ oz. flour	a little salt
½ pt milk	

Cook the chicory as in the previous recipe. Strain. Melt the fat in a saucepan, add the flour and stew for 2 to 3 mins., stirring all the time. Add the stock or water and the milk and boil for another 5 mins., still stirring. Add the marmite and salt. This is now the marmite sauce to which the chicory is added. Heat up and serve.

Braised Chicory. For 4

1 lb. chicory	1½ tsp. yeast extract
2 oz. butter or fat	1 bayleaf
1 Tbs. cornflour	2 peppercorns
½ pt stock or water	salt to taste

Cook the chicory as for boiled. Then carry on exactly as for Braised Celery from the second paragraph (page 57).

Chicory with Tomatoes and Mushrooms. For 4

¾ lb. chicory	1 medium onion
¼ lb. mushrooms	2 oz. fat
½ lb. tomatoes	salt to taste

Cook the chicory as for boiled. Wash the tomatoes and cut them in half. Wash and slice the mushrooms. Peel and chop the onion. Now melt 1 oz. fat in a saucepan, add the chicory and stew for about 10 mins. without water. Fry the onion and mushrooms separately in the remaining fat for 5 to 10 mins. and keep hot. Add the tomatoes to the chicory and stew for another 5 to 10 mins. Finally mix the onion and mushrooms carefully into the chicory-tomato mixture and serve.

Corn on the Cob. For 4

4 large or 8 small corncobs	2 oz. butter
water to cover	

Remove the outer leaves and silky strands from the cobs, trim the stem closely. Bring enough water to the boil to cover the cobs and cook for 5 mins. (never longer than 7 mins.). If they are not very young and fresh, a little sugar added to the cooking water is useful. If the corn is hard, no amount of cooking will soften them. Strain them, place them on large dish, and pour the melted butter over them.

NOTE. The cooking water is very good for stock, but very fresh cobs can also be eaten raw.

Creamed Mixed Greens. For 4

2 lb. mixed green leaves*
Béchamel Sauce (page 96)

Wash all the leaves carefully, rinse them under running water, and strip off any brown parts and rough stalks. Cut coarsely and boil in enough water to cover them until tender. Then strain, chop finely and mix with a béchamel sauce.

Kale (Curly Kale) à la Béchamel. For 4

2 lb. kale	½ pt stock or water
1 medium onion	½ pt milk or water
2 oz. fat	½ tsp. yeast extract
1½ oz. flour	1 tsp. sugar
a little nutmeg and salt to taste	

Strip the curly leaves off the stalks and wash them several times, once under running water. Boil with 1 cup water (or stock) until the kale is soft. Strain and chop the leaves finely (see under Spinach, page 68). Peel and chop the onion finely and stew it in a saucepan with 1½ oz. fat until golden brown. Add the flour and stew for 2 to 3 mins., then add milk and stock (or water from the cooked kale) and cook for another 5 mins., stirring all the time. Add the chopped kale, yeast extract, sugar, salt, and nutmeg, heat up again and finally stir in the remaining ½ oz. fat and serve.

NOTE. The cooking time is slightly reduced and the flavour improved if the kale has been exposed to frost.

* Any of the following can be used: cauliflower leaves, green broccoli, outside cabbage and lettuce leaves, turnip tops, tops of beetroots, radishes, etc. Note that broccoli and lettuce leaves tend to give the dish a slightly bitter flavour, so use with discrimination.

Boiled Leeks. For 4

    2 lb. leeks
    a little salt to taste

Remove the roots and any damaged outer leaves. Cut the leeks
lengthwise in halves and wash carefully. Rinse under running
water, opening up the outer leaves a little so that the water can
penetrate. Cut once or twice across. Start cooking without adding water as enough washing water will cling to the leeks. This
will soon disappear, and at this point add ½ cup of water and
cook until the leeks are quite soft.

Braised Leeks. For 4

    2 lb. leeks   1½ tsp. yeast extract
    1½ oz. butter or fat   1 bayleaf
    1 Tbs. cornflour   2 peppercorns
    ½ pt stock or water   salt to taste

Prepare and boil leeks as in previous recipe. Then carry on
exactly as for Braised Celery from the second paragraph (page 57).

Leeks au Gratin. For 4

    2 lb. leeks   Cheese Sauce (page 97)
    ½ oz. butter   1½ oz. grated cheese

Prepare and boil the leeks, strain and keep hot. Place the leeks
in a buttered fireproof dish. Make a cheese sauce, pour over the
leeks, sprinkle grated cheese on top, and bake in a moderate
oven (350°, Reg. 4–5) for 30 mins.

Creamed Leeks and Carrots. For 4

    1 lb. leeks   ½ tsp. yeast extract
    1 lb. carrots   Cream Sauce (page 95)
    1 oz. fat or butter   salt to taste

Cook the leeks as for boiled and strain. Peel and slice the carrots
thinly. Melt the fat in a saucepan and stew the carrots in it
gently until they are tender, adding if necessary one or two Tbs.
water or stock. Make a cream sauce and add the yeast extract.
Mix the vegetables into the sauce, heat up and serve.

Lettuce. For 4

2 medium Cos lettuces
1 oz. butter or fat

Trim off the stem and cut the lettuce in quarters. Wash it several times, once under running water. Bring 1 cup of water to boil, add the lettuce, and cook for 5 to 10 mins. Drain (the water cannot be used further), melt the fat and pour it over the lettuce.

Lettuce au Gratin. For 4

2 medium Cos lettuces   Cheese Sauce (page 97)
1 oz. butter or fat   2 oz. grated cheese

Cook the lettuce as in previous recipe, drain, and cool. Then cut each quarter again lengthwise and roll each piece tightly into a roll. Butter a fireproof dish with half the fat and place the lettuce rolls in it neatly. Make the cheese sauce, pour it over the lettuce rolls, sprinkle the grated cheese on top, and finally place the remaining fat, cut into small pieces, on top. Bake in hot oven (450°, Reg. 6–7) for 30 mins.

Steamed Marrow. For 4

2–3 lb. marrow $\frac{1}{2}$ cup water or stock
chopped parsley   salt to taste

If the marrow is very young, clean it with a scrubbing brush and top and tail it. If it is not so young, peel it, cut it in half, and scrape out pips and membranes. In both cases cut it into large cubes, cook them in $\frac{1}{2}$ cup stock or water until tender (about 10 mins.), and serve with chopped parsley.

Stewed Marrow. For 4

2–3 lb. marrow   1 oz. fat or butter
1 small onion   chopped parsley

Prepare the marrow as in the previous recipe. Peel and cube the onion. Melt the fat in a saucepan, add the onion, stew for 2 mins., add the marrow cubes and stew for about 10 mins. Do not add any water. Serve with chopped parsley.

Fried Marrows. For 4

2–3 lb. young marrows
2 oz. butter or fat

Use only small young marrows for this. Scrub, top and tail, and cut into slices, not too thick. Melt the fat in a large frying pan and fry the marrow slices until slightly brown.

Creamed Marrows. For 4

2 lb. marrow   Cream Sauce (page 95)
chopped parsley

Cook the marrow as for steamed. Make the cream sauce. Mix both together and serve with chopped parsley.

Marrows au Gratin. For 4

2 lb. marrow   Cheese Sauce (page 97)
½ oz. fat   2 oz. grated cheese

Prepare and cook the marrow as for steamed. Make the cheese sauce. Place the cooked marrows mixed with the cheese sauce in a buttered fireproof dish, top with the grated cheese and bake in a moderate oven (350°, Reg. 4) for about 30 mins.

Marrows with Tomato Sauce. For 4

2 lb. marrow   Tomato Sauce (page 101)
chopped chives or parsley

Cook the marrow as for steamed. Make the tomato sauce. Before serving mix both together and top with chopped parsley and/or chives.

Marrows with Mushroom Sauce. For 4

Exactly as previous recipe, but with Mushroom Sauce (page 100) instead of Tomato Sauce.

Marrows with Sauce Hollandaise. For 4

2 lb. marrow
Sauce Hollandaise (page 98)

Cook the marrow as for steamed. Make the sauce hollandaise.
Serve the marrows and sauce separately.

Marrows with Fresh Tomatoes. For 4

2 lb. marrow	¼ pt stock or water
½ lb. tomatoes	1 oz. fat
1 small onion	½ bayleaf

Prepare (but do not cook) the marrow as for steamed. Cut the
tomatoes in half and chop the onion. Melt the fat in a saucepan,
add the onion and tomatoes and stew for about 5 to 7 mins.
Add the marrow cubes and the stock (or water) and cook gently
in a covered saucepan until the marrows are soft (20 to 30 mins.).
Serve with chopped parsley.

Stewed Mushrooms. For 4

1 lb. mushrooms	1½ oz. fat or butter
½ lb. onions	chopped parsley

Wash the mushrooms carefully and strain. Cut them into thin
slices (do not peel). Chop the peeled onions. Melt the butter or
fat in a frying pan (preferably one with a high rim), add the
onions and stew for 2 to 3 mins., then add the sliced mushrooms
(no water) and stew for a further 10 mins. Serve with chopped
parsley.

Fried Mushrooms. For 4

Use the same ingredients and method as in the previous recipe
but stew the mushrooms longer, drain off any excess liquid, and
fry until brown.

Creamed Mushrooms. For 4

1 lb. mushrooms	½ tsp. yeast extract
½ lb. onions	Cream Sauce (page 95)

Stew the mushrooms. Make a cream sauce; add the yeast extract,
and mix both together. Serve with chopped parsley.

Grilled Mushrooms. For 4 small helpings

1¼ lb. mushrooms	2 Tbs. apple juice or water
1 oz. fat or butter	a little salt to taste

Wash the mushrooms carefully; if they are small leave them whole, otherwise cut them into halves. Put the water or apple juice and fat into the grill pan, without the grid, and heat under the grill until it boils, stirring in order to blend the fat and liquid. Put the mushrooms into this mixture and grill the top, then turn them over and grill the other side, seeing that the mushrooms are well coated with the liquid which they will have absorbed by the time they are done.

Mushrooms and Tomatoes Niçoise. For 4

1 lb. mushrooms	1½ oz. butter or oil
1 lb. tomatoes	1 clove of garlic or
1 small onion	¼ tsp. garlic salt

Wash the mushrooms, and leave them whole (cut the really big ones in half). Wash the tomatoes and cut them in half. Peel and chop the onion. Stew the onion in the butter or oil for 2 to 3 mins., add the tomatoes and stew for another 5 mins., then add the mushrooms and stew for another 10 mins. Add the garlic salt now, stir in well and stew for one more minute. If real garlic is used, a clove should be chopped finely and stewed together with the onion.

Boiled Onions. For 4

12–16 medium onions

Trim and peel the onions. Cook whole in just enough water to cover them for ¾ to 1 hour. Strain and serve. Add a little butter if desired.

Braised Onions. For 4

12–16 medium onions	Cream Sauce (page 95)
2 oz. fat	2 tsp. yeast extract

Trim and peel the onions and cook them in boiling water for about 5 mins. Strain. Melt 1½ oz. fat in a fireproof dish and place the onions upright in it. Melt the remaining fat in a small saucepan and paint each onion with this fat. Bake in a hot oven (400°, Reg. 6) for 30 to 45 mins. The onions should be soft but not mashy. Make the sauce and add the yeast extract, pour it over the onions, and bake for another 5 mins. Serve at once.

Baked Onions. For 4

12–16 medium onions

Trim and wash, but do not peel, the onions. Put them upright on to a fireproof dish and bake for 45 mins. to 1 hour (large onions take longer) in a hot oven (400 – 425°, Reg. 6 or 7). When they are ready they will be soft to the touch.

Steamed Parsnips. For 4

1½ lb. parsnips

Trim, wash, and peel the parsnips. Cut into cubes or 1-inch strips. Boil in very little water (½ cup) until tender. Strain. Toss in melted butter if desired.

Parsnips à la Béchamel. For 4

1½ lb. parsnips   Béchamel Sauce (page 96)
chopped parsley

Prepare and boil the parsnips as in previous recipe. Make the béchamel sauce and mix with the cooked parsnips. Serve with chopped parsley sprinkled on top.

Parsnips Sauté. For 4

1½ lb. parsnips
2 oz. fat

Trim, wash, and peel the parsnips. If they are small leave them whole, otherwise halve or quarter them. Boil them in a cupful of water until nearly soft. Strain and cool; then cut them into ½-inch cubes. Melt the fat in a frying pan and fry the parsnips until they are slightly brown. Serve at once.

Mashed Parsnips. For 4

1 lb. parsnips	1 onion
½ lb. potatoes	1½ oz. fat or butter

Prepare the parsnips as in previous recipe and boil them until they are quite soft. Peel the potatoes and boil them with a little salt until they are quite soft. Strain both vegetables and mash them separately; then mix them together with 1 oz. fat. Peel and chop the onion, and fry in the remaining fat until golden brown. Heat up the parsnip mixture and serve on a plate, topped with the fried onions.

Boiled Garden Peas. For 4

2 lb. peas	1 cup water
salt, sugar, mint to taste	

Shell the peas (the pods are excellent for vegetable stock). Put them into the cold water and boil for about 20 mins. Add a little salt and sugar to the water, also some mint leaves if desired.

Peas and Carrots à la Crème. For 4

Similar to Carrots and Peas à la Crème (page 54) but use more peas than carrots, say 1¾ lb. peas and ½ lb. carrots. The method of preparation is exactly the same.

Peas and Lettuce (boiled). For 4

1½ lb. peas	½ small onion
1 small Cos lettuce	1 oz. fat

Shell and boil peas. Wash the lettuce carefully. Then cut it across, into 1 inch strips. Melt the fat in a saucepan, add the onions and lettuce and stew until tender. Mix this with the peas and add a little water if the vegetables are too dry. Serve with a few mint leaves if desired.

Peas and Onions. For 4

1½ lb. peas	½ pt milk, water, or stock
4–6 small onions*	sugar and salt to taste
1 oz. fat	

* Better still for this dish are ½ lb. 'pearl' onions (normally used for pickling) if they are obtainable instead of the ordinary onions.

Cook peas as for boiled and strain. Peel the onions and stew whole in the fat until quite tender. If the onions start sticking add a little of the liquid. (Milk is preferable as its taste blends well with that of the onions.) Mix together with the peas and add the remaining liquid. Reheat and serve.

Pepper. See page 79.

Pumpkin

This is best known used in sweets; as a vegetable it can be cooked like marrows (pages 61–3) or roasted in the oven (next recipe). The pips can be dried, peeled, and then used like nuts for cakes and salads, etc.

Roasted Pumpkin. For 4

2 lb. pumpkin	a little water or
1 oz. fat	vegetable stock

Peel the pumpkin and take out the inside (pips, membranes, pith, etc.). Cut the fleshy part into large pieces and put into a buttered fireproof dish. Add a little stock or water and roast in hot oven (400°, Reg. 6) until quite soft.

Salsify or Oyster Plant. See page 81.

Seakale. See page 82.

Buttered Leaf Spinach. For 4

2 lb. spinach	salt and nutmeg to taste
2 oz. butter	

Pick the spinach over carefully, removing weeds, seeds, and decayed leaves. Wash several times, at least once under running water which should eventually be absolutely clear. Cook with only that water which clings to the spinach after washing. Do not overcook; 5 mins. boiling is normally sufficient. Strain and gently press out the surplus water left in the spinach. Melt the butter, return the spinach into the saucepan and toss in the butter. Add salt and nutmeg to taste. Serve at once.

Creamed Spinach. For 4

2 lb. spinach   grated nutmeg and salt to taste
Cream Sauce (page 95)

Cook spinach as in the previous recipe. When it is soft, strain it
and either chop it finely or put it through a mincer. Make a
cream sauce, mix in the chopped or minced spinach, and add a
little grated nutmeg and salt to taste.

Spinach à la Béchamel. For 4

Exactly as previous recipe but with Béchamel Sauce (page 96)
instead of cream sauce.

Boiled Swedes. For 4

2 lb. swedes   salt to taste
2 oz. butter (optional)

Scrub the swedes and peel thickly. Cut into 1 inch cubes and
boil in very little water, about 1 cup, until soft. The time depends
on the age of the swedes, and will be 10 to 20 mins. Strain. If you
want to improve the taste (and add to the calories) melt 2 oz.
butter in a saucepan and toss the swedes in it. Add salt to taste.

Swedes à la Crème. For 4

2 lb. swedes   chopped parsley
Cream Sauce (page 95)   salt to taste

Cook the swedes as in the previous recipe. Strain. Some of the
water can be used for making the cream sauce. Mix the sauce
and swedes together, add salt to taste, top with chopped parsley,
and serve.

Mashed Swedes. For 4

1½ lb. swedes   1 small onion
½ lb. potatoes   2 oz. fat or butter

Cook the swedes as for boiled until very soft. Peel the potatoes
and boil until also very soft. Mash swedes and potatoes separately. Melt 1 oz. fat in a saucepan, put the mashed swedes and
potatoes in, heat over a low flame and whisk, preferably with a

strong egg whisk. Peel and chop the onion and fry in the remaining fat until golden brown. Pour the fried onions over the mashed vegetables just before serving.

Swedes Sauté. For 4

2 lb. swedes
2 oz. oil

Cook swedes as for boiled, strain and cool. Then heat the oil in a frying pan and fry the swedes until light brown. Serve at once.

Tomatoes (Stewed or Baked). For 4

2 lb. tomatoes
1 oz. fat or butter

Remove the 'flower' and wash the tomatoes. They need not be skinned if washed thoroughly. (Although they may look clean, tomatoes are often sprayed with chemicals which should be washed off.) Either leave them whole or cut them in half.

Stewed: Melt the fat in a saucepan, put the tomatoes in, add a little salt, and stew 5 to 10 mins. until tender.

Baked. Grease a fireproof dish and place the tomatoes in it. If used whole cut a cross in the top or prick them to prevent them from bursting. Bake for 20 mins. in a moderate oven (300°, Reg. 3).

Fried Tomatoes. For 4

2 lb. tomatoes
1 large onion

2 oz. oil
salt to taste

Prepare the tomatoes as in the previous recipe; cut in half. Peel the onion and cut into rings. Heat the oil in a frying pan, put the onions in and fry for about 2 mins., then add the tomatoes and fry for another 10 mins. If served on toast or as an additional vegetable a slightly smaller quantity may be used.

Scalloped Tomatoes. For 4

1½ lb. large tomatoes
1 medium onion
½ oz. fat

3 oz. breadcrumbs
2 oz. grated cheese
chopped parsley

Peel, chop, and fry the onions in the fat. Mix them with the breadcrumbs and half the grated cheese. Grease a fireproof dish, put in first a layer of sliced tomatoes, then a layer of breadcrumb mixture, then tomatoes and so forth, finishing with a layer of the breadcrumb mixture. Top this with the remaining grated cheese (and, if desired, with a few knobs of butter) and bake in a hot oven (400°, Reg. 6) for 30 to 35 mins.

Steamed Turnips. For 4

2 lb. turnips   chopped parsley
1 oz. butter (optional)   1 cup water

Wash and peel the turnips. Cut them into small cubes or thin slices. If they are very young leave them whole. Boil them in 1 cup of water until they are soft, 8 to 10 mins. Strain them and serve them with chopped parsley. If butter is used, melt it in a saucepan, add the parsley and the hot turnips and toss until everything is well mixed. Serve at once.

Turnips with Brown Sauce. For 4

2 lb. turnips
Brown Sauce (page 100)

Cook the turnips as in the previous recipe. Strain. Make the Brown Sauce and mix the turnips into it.

Turnips with Tomato Sauce. For 4

Exactly as the previous recipe with Tomato Sauce (page 101) instead of Brown Sauce.

Turnip Tops à la Crème. For 4

2 lb. turnip tops
Cream Sauce (page 95)

Pick over the turnip tops carefully, discard all discoloured leaves, then wash them carefully, at least once under running water. Cook them with a cup of water or stock until tender, 10 to 20 mins. Strain and chop finely. Make a cream sauce and mix with the chopped turnip tops.

Turnip Tops à la Béchamel. For 4

Exactly as previous recipe with Béchamel Sauce (page 96) instead of Cream Sauce.

VEGETABLES EN CASSEROLE

A casserole is a fireproof dish with a well-fitting lid. It can be made of enamelled cast iron, earthenware, or fireproof glass. Casserole-cooked vegetables taste richer because all the juices (including the minerals and trace elements) are kept intact although because of the longer cooking time some of the vitamins get lost. This type of cooking is particularly useful for winter vegetables which require longer cooking anyway. The vegetables can be served in the casserole, and will in this way keep hot longer.

Greasing the casserole always includes greasing the lid.

Jerusalem Artichoke Casserole. For 4

1 lb. artichokes	1 oz. fat.
2 medium carrots	½ pt stock or water
1 large onion	salt to taste

Prepare the artichokes as for Steamed Jerusalem Artichokes (page 43). Peel the carrots and onions. Cut the vegetables into medium-thick slices. Grease the casserole and put in alternate layers of artichokes, carrots, and onions, finishing with artichokes, and putting the fat between the layers. Pour the stock over and cook in a hot oven (400°, Reg. 6) for about an hour.

Carrot, Onion, and Potato Casserole. For 4

½ lb. carrots	1 tsp. yeast extract
½ lb. potatoes	1 small tsp. dried marjoram or
2 large onions	equivalent fresh
1 oz. fat	salt to taste
½ pt stock or water	

Wash and peel the vegetables and cut them into medium-thick slices. Melt the fat in the casserole and stir in the vegetables to cover them thoroughly with fat. Add a little salt and marjoram. Mix the yeast extract with the heated stock (or water) and pour over the vegetables. Cook in a hot oven (400°, Reg. 6) for an hour.

Vegetable Hot Pot. For 4

2 carrots	a few runner beans (if in season)
1 large turnip	1 pt stock
2 leeks	2 onions
1 small head celery	1 tsp. yeast extract
½ lb. potatoes	salt to taste
1½ oz. fat	

Prepare the vegetables as in the previous recipe, the leeks and celery being cut in ½ inch pieces. Melt 1 oz. fat in a casserole and put all the vegetables except the potatoes in it. Stir well in order to cover them with fat. Mix the yeast extract and salt into the heated stock (or water) and pour over the vegetables. Now cut the potatoes into thin slices, arrange them on top of the vegetables and dab the remaining fat on them. Cover and cook for about 45 mins. in a hot oven (400°, Reg. 6), with a further 15 mins. without the lid to brown the potatoes.

Broad Bean Casserole (Bean Cassoulet). For 4

1½ lb. broad beans	2 oz. fat
1 large carrot	½ pt stock or water
1 leek	a few leaves summer savory or
1 onion	equivalent dried

Cook the beans as on page 46. Peel and slice the carrot and onion. Wash and cut the leeks into ½ inch pieces. Melt ½ oz. fat in a saucepan and stew the vegetables except the beans for about 5 mins. Add no water. Grease a casserole and put in alternate layers of beans and other vegetables, finishing with beans and putting the remaining fat between the layers. Mix the stock with the savory (fresh or dried) and a little salt and pour over the vegetables. Cook in a hot oven (400°, Reg. 6) for 35 mins.

Marrow, Tomato, and Onion Casserole. For 4

1 lb. vegetable marrow	1½ oz. fat
1 lb. tomatoes	½ pt stock or water
½ lb. onions	2 tsp. tomato purée

Wash the tomatoes and cut into thick slices. Peel and slice the onions. Prepare the marrows as for Steamed Marrow (page 61). Grease a casserole and put in first a layer of tomatoes, then one of onions, then of marrows and repeat, putting the fat between the layers. The last layer should be marrows. Mix the tomato purée and a little salt with the stock (or water) and pour over the vegetables. Cook in a hot oven (400°, Reg. 6) for an hour.

The recipes we have given are proved favourites. However, variations in the vegetables used, depending on your taste or on what is available, are possible and perfectly simple to do, as long as you follow the basic method used in these recipes.

UNUSUAL VEGETABLES AND COMBINATIONS

Globe Artichokes

These are Mediterranean and sub-tropical plants, but the smaller, spiky type are now also grown in Kent. The flower head, not fully developed, contains the delicious edible artichoke bottom (*fond d'artichaut*), the outer leaves or petals which are also partly edible – and the hairy 'choke' which is not.

To eat an artichoke, pull the leaves away, using your fingers, dip them in the sauce, and suck out the fleshy part (rather like the way asparagus is eaten). Then discard the 'choke' and eat the *fond*, also with the sauce. Sometimes only artichoke bottoms are used.

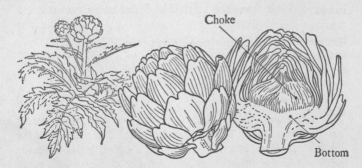

Choke

Bottom

Steamed Globe Artichokes

Allow one large or two small artichokes per person. Wash them
thoroughly, at least once under running water. Trim off the
stem at the bottom and remove any outer leaves which are hard
or brown. Cook the artichokes in boiling water with a little salt
for ¾ to 1 hour. They are done if the outer leaves come off easily
when pulled lightly.

Serve with: Mayonnaise (page 170); Sauce Hollandaise (page
98); any other piquant sauce (e.g. page 101). Very tasty, too,
cold with Vinaigrette (page 171).

Aubergines (Egg Plants)

The egg-shaped fruit of this tropical plant has a shiny skin, purple
to black. Some rarer varieties are of different colour.

Stewed Aubergines. For 4

2 large or 3 small	1 clove garlic
aubergines	salt or garlic salt
2 oz. oil	chopped parsley

Trim off the leaves, wash the aubergines, and dry with a towel,
but do not peel. Cut into 1 inch cubes. Stew the finely chopped
garlic in the oil for 1 min. Add the aubergine cubes and stew
until soft. This may take anything from 5 to 20 mins., depending
on how ripe the aubergines were when they were picked and
how long they were in transit – or in the shop. Sprinkle some
chopped parsley over the finished dish and serve at once.

Aubergines and Tomatoes Provençale. For 4

2 aubergines	2 oz. oil
½ lb. tomatoes	garlic salt or
1 small onion	1 clove of garlic
chopped parsley	salt to taste

Prepare the aubergines as in previous recipe. Wash the tomatoes
and cut them in half. Peel the onion and cut it in rings. Heat the
oil in a saucepan, mix with the finely chopped garlic (or garlic
salt), put in the onion rings and stew for another 5 to 8 mins.

Finally, add the tomatoes and aubergines and stew for another
10 mins. Serve with chopped parsley.

Beignets of Aubergines. For 4

2 aubergines	1 clove garlic
beignet mixture (page 132)	oil for deep frying

Wash the aubergines and cut them into ¼-inch slices. Rub each
slice with garlic, then dip it into the beignet mixture and fry in
deep fat until golden brown.

Aubergines Polonaise. For 4

2 aubergines	garlic salt
1 egg*	breadcrumbs
½ cup milk	fat for deep frying

Wash the aubergines and cut them into ¼-inch slices. Whisk the
egg, milk, and garlic salt together. Dip each slice of aubergine
into the egg mixture and roll in breadcrumbs so that the slices
are well covered. Fry in deep fat until golden brown.

Cardoons

These are related to the globe artichokes (see page 73), but
whereas the artichokes are grown for their edible flower heads
the cardoons are grown for their edible leaf stalks. They are
cooked in the same ways as celery (see page 55), but be careful
to remove all the stringy parts.

Celeriac

This is the turnip-shaped root of a special variety of celery
plant. It is extremely popular on the Continent, where our type
of celery is known as 'English celery'.

Steamed Celeriac

1 large celeriac or 8 oz. per person

Scrub and peel the celeriac. (The peel is excellent for stock.)
Cut it into ½-inch slices or cubes and cook it gently in a saucepan

* 1 tsp. soya flour can be used instead of the egg.

with a cup of water until soft. This may take up to an hour, so
make sure the saucepan does not run dry.

Celeriac Sauté. For 4

1 large celeriac   2 pt water
2 Tbs. oil   salt to taste

Scrub but do not peel the celeriac; cut it in quarters. Cook it in
2 pt water for about 30 mins., i.e. not quite soft. Take it out,
peel it, and cut it into ½-inch cubes. Fry the celeriac cubes in the
oil until they are golden brown.

Celeriac au Gratin. For 4

1 large or 2 small celeriac   1 oz. grated cheese
1 oz. fat or butter   salt to taste
Cheese Sauce (page 97)

Cook the celeriac as for steamed. Strain and mix with the cheese
sauce. Put this mixture into a fireproof dish, sprinkle 1 oz.
grated cheese on top and bake for 30 mins. in a hot oven (400°,
Reg. 6–7).

Fried Celeriac Polonaise. For 4

1 celeriac (medium root)   oil for deep frying
1 large egg   breadcrumbs
2 Tbs. milk   salt to taste

Scrub the celeriac and boil it with the peel until it is fairly, but
not quite, soft. Then peel and cut it into ½-inch thick slices.
Beat the egg, milk, and salt together, dip the celeriac slices into
it, cover them with breadcrumbs, and fry in deep fat (oil) until
golden brown.

Fennel

Fennel is grown in the same way as celery (the lower part of
the fleshy, tightly packed leaves is kept under ground), mainly
in France (*fenouil*) and Italy (*finocci*). The leaves are used as a
culinary herb. As a vegetable it is particularly appreciated by
those who like its strong aniseed flavour.

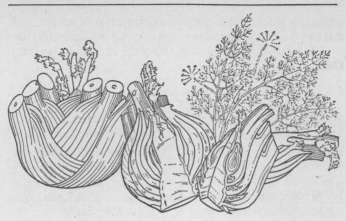

Steamed Fennel. For 4

4 fennel plants
2 oz. butter (optional)

Wash the fennel and strip or cut off any brown parts, and the feathery green leaves on top, which can be used for flavouring sauces. Put enough water in a saucepan to cover the fennel but bring the water to the boil before putting the fennel in. Cook until soft, 15 to 30 mins., then strain and serve. It can also be served after being tossed in melted butter.

Fennel au Gratin. For 4

4 fennel plants   3 Tbs. cream
2 oz. grated cheese   1 oz. butter or fat

Prepare the fennel as in the previous recipe, cut it in half lengthwise, and cook as above. Then grease (butter preferably) a fireproof dish, place the fennel in it, pour on the cream, sprinkle with grated cheese, and put little knobs of butter on top. Bake in a medium oven (325°, Reg. 4) until the top is brown.

Kohlrabi

This is a kind of cabbage with a turnip-shaped stem. According to the Oxford dictionary 'it is used in England as food for cattle'. Its taste is much more delicate than that of turnips, and it is one of those inexplicable things that in this country it is not used much more as a delicious vegetable, as it is on the continent.

Creamed Kohlrabi Béchamel. For 4

2 lb. kohlrabi, with or without the leaves
Béchamel Sauce (page 96)

nutmeg, sugar, and salt to taste
1 oz. fat

First remove the leaves, if any. (Sometimes the kohlrabi are available only without leaves. In this case, just leave them out!) The tough outside leaves can be used for stock, the tender inside leaves are cooked, after thorough washing, in just enough water to cover them. Strain and chop them finely. Peel the tuberous part, the actual kohlrabi, and cut it into thin slices. Melt the fat in a saucepan and stew these slices in it for 5 to 10 mins., shaking the saucepan occasionally to prevent them from sticking; then keep them hot. Make a béchamel sauce and mix in the chopped up leaves and, carefully, the kohlrabi slices. Add a little salt, sugar, and nutmeg to taste.

Stewed Kohlrabi. For 4

2 lb. kohlrabi
  (without the leaves)
1½ oz. fat

salt to taste
parsley (optional)

Wash and peel the kohlrabi and cut into thin slices or small cubes. Melt the fat in a saucepan and add the kohlrabi. Stew for about 5 mins. (or until soft). Add salt to taste and serve at once. Chopped parsley can be added.

Stuffed Kohlrabi. For 4

4 kohlrabis
  (medium-size)
Stuffing
2 oz. bread
¾ cup milk
½ small onion
1 oz. mushrooms
½ oz. fat

½ pt stock or water
1 oz. grated cheese

½ oz. grated cheese
herbs (marjoram or tarragon)
1 small egg
garlic or garlic salt

Prepare the stuffing as on page 116 (Cabbage Roulade) but using the quantities given here. With a spoon or potato scooper scoop enough out of each kohlrabi to make room for 1 to 1½ Tbs. of filling. Grease a casserole and place the stuffed kohlrabis in it, add the stock, and top with grated cheese. Cover the casserole and bake in a hot oven (450°, Reg. 7) for about an hour; the cheese on top should by then be brown.

Green or Sweet Peppers

Also known as Capsicums, Pimentoes, or Pepperoni, they are becoming increasingly popular and are seen more and more at good greengrocers; they are fairly fleshy, smooth-skinned fruits, usually bright green (but sometimes also bright yellow or red). With their peculiar flavour they are a very useful vegetable as a main dish, as in any of the following recipes, but also as additions to and flavouring for soups and salads (cooked or raw) as well as for stews and casseroles.

The seeds should always be removed. They can be frightfully hot and may easily spoil the dish.

Peppers with Tomatoes. For 4

4 large peppers	1 clove garlic or garlic salt
1 lb. tomatoes	1 bayleaf
1 small onion	chopped parsley
2 oz. oil	

Wash the peppers and cut them in half. Remove the inner membranes and seeds. Make sure that the seeds are all removed by rinsing under running water. Cut the peppers into thin slices. Cut the tomatoes in half. Peel and chop the onions and garlic clove. Heat the oil in a saucepan, add the onions and garlic (or garlic salt), and stew for 2 to 3 mins. Then add the sliced peppers and stew for another 5 mins., add the tomatoes and the bayleaf. Another 5 mins. will be needed to soften all the vegetables. Stir from time to time to prevent sticking. Serve with chopped parsley.

Peppers

Salsify and Scorzonera

They are grown nearly everywhere for their edible roots. For cooking there is no difference between the two.

Salsify is sometimes called oyster plant or vegetable oyster; scorzonera is sometimes called black salsify because its roots are darker, almost black, hence its German name *Schwarzwurzel* (= black root). When peeled the roots of both varieties are white.

Steamed Salsify. For 4

2 lb. salsify
2 oz. butter (optional)

Wash and peel the salsify. Immediately after peeling rub the white root with a little lemon juice to prevent it from discolouring. Cut into 2-inch pieces and boil them in just enough water to cover, having added a few drops of lemon juice to the cooking water. Strain when soft, and serve. To improve the dish, toss the cooked salsify in 2 oz. of melted butter.

Salsify à la Crème. For 4

2 lb. salsify
chopped parsley
Cream Sauce (page 95) made
  with salsify water

Cook the salsify as in the previous recipe and make a cream sauce using part of the salsify

cooking water for it. Mix the chopped parsley into the sauce and then the cooked salsify.

Salsify à la Hollandaise. For 4

2 lb. salsify
Sauce Hollandaise (page 98)

Exactly as previous recipe with Hollandaise instead of Cream Sauce and no parsley. Salsify blends extremely well with sauce hollandaise. An alternative would be to serve the sauce separately.

Salsify and Peas à la Crème. For 4

1 lb. salsify   Cream Sauce (page 95)
1 lb. green peas   1 tsp. chopped mint
juice of half a lemon   salt to taste

Cook the salsify as for steamed and the peas as for boiled (page 66). Strain both vegetables and keep them hot. Make a cream sauce using part of the salsify and pea water. Add the chopped mint and lemon juice to the sauce and mix the vegetables into it.

Seakale

These are the young white shoots of a plant belonging to the cabbage family. It is in season in this country from late December till February.

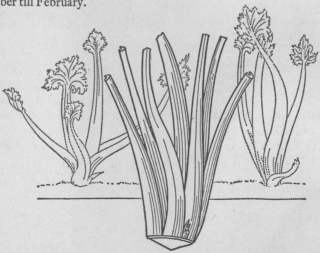

Steamed Seakale. For 4

1½ lb. seakale   2 oz. butter (optional)
1 tsp. lemon juice   salt to taste

Cut off any discoloured leaves and either peel or cut off the
stump. Wash thoroughly and bunch several pieces together
with tape or cotton to make handling easier. Cook in boiling
water for about 20 mins. until tender. (A skewer is a good instru-
ment for testing this.) Strain, cut the tapes, and pour the lemon
juice over the seakale just before serving. You can, if you like,
pour 2 oz. melted butter over it as well.

Seakale à la Crème. For 4

1½ lb. seakale
Cream Sauce (page 95)

Cook the seakale as in the previous recipe. Make a cream sauce,
pour it over the hot seakale, and serve.

Seakale Bordelaise. For 4

Same as previous recipe but with Bordelaise Sauce (page 96)
instead of Cream Sauce.

Seakale Hollandaise. For 4

Same as Seakale à la Crème but with Hollandaise Sauce (page
98) instead of Cream Sauce. The sauce should in this case be
served separately.

Samphire

Described sometimes as a seaweed, samphire is in fact a cliff
plant which will thrive even inland if given some salt water. In its
pickled form it used to be very popular in coastal areas where
the plants are obtainable rather from the fishmonger than from
the greengrocer. Only the fleshy parts from the leaves are edible
and only really fresh plants should be used for cooking.

Buttered Samphire. For 4

2–3 lb. samphire
2 oz. butter

Wash and remove any leaves which are not quite fresh and perhaps even slimy. Put the samphire in about 2 pt boiling water and cook for about half an hour. Take it out carefully and serve it with melted or hot brown butter.

To eat it, suck the fleshy parts from the stringy leaf veins – using your fingers (rather in the same way as asparagus).

Sauerkraut (Choucroute)

This is often wrongly described as pickled cabbage. It is really shredded white cabbage which has been kept under slight pressure in brine, where after some months it has turned slightly sour without the addition of any acid. This is the real sauerkraut. The tinned variety may have some chemical acids added as a preservative.

Fried Sauerkraut. For 4

1½ lb. sauerkraut   2 oz. fat or oil
1 medium onion

Wash the sauerkraut to remove any excess brine. If tinned sauerkraut is used wash it thoroughly with warm water. Fry the chopped onion in the fat or oil for about 2 mins., then add the sauerkraut and fry for another 5 to 10 mins., loosening the sauerkraut with a fork from time to time. Add a little stock or water, cover with a lid and stew over a low flame for another 10 to 15 mins., stirring from time to time. Cooked in this way it is easy to digest.

Sauerkraut Potato Dish (Pommes Mousseline à la Choucroute). For 4

¾ lb. sauerkraut   mashed potatoes from
1 oz. fat   1½ lb. potatoes (page 111)
1 small onion   a little beaten egg

Prepare sauerkraut as in previous recipe up to 'loosening the sauerkraut with a fork from time to time'. Grease a fireproof dish, put in a layer of half the mashed potatoes, then a layer of the fried sauerkraut and finally another layer with the rest of the mashed potatoes. Paint the top with a little beaten egg and add a few small knobs of butter or fat. Bake in a moderate oven (350°, Reg. 4–5) for 30 to 45 mins. and serve at once.

COMPOSITE VEGETABLE DISHES

Beetroot Ragoût. For 4

1 lb. cooked beetroots	½ pt stock or water
1 large onion	1½ oz. flour
1 large cooking apple	1 bayleaf
½ lb. boiled potatoes	2 Tbs. vinegar or
3–4 gherkins	lemon juice
1 tsp. capers	½ Tbs. sugar
1 oz. fat	chopped parsley
3–4 Tbs. sour cream (optional)	

Peel the beetroots and onions. Cut the beetroots and potatoes into ½ inch cubes and chop the onions. Peel and cube the apple. Melt the fat in a saucepan and fry the onions until golden brown; add the flour and stew for 2 to 3 mins., stirring all the time. Add the stock or water and stew for another 5 mins. Then add the vinegar (or lemon juice), sugar, a little salt to taste, bayleaf, capers, and chopped gherkins. Finally mix in the apple, beetroots, and potatoes, heat up and simmer for at least 10 mins., stirring from time to time. Just before serving remove the bayleaf, and top with chopped parsley, and, if you like, sour cream.

Broad Bean Stew. For 4

2 lb. broad beans	1 pt stock or water
2 large onions	1 oz. fat
1 large carrot	1 tsp. dried savory or
2 sticks celery	equivalent fresh

Cook the beans as on page 46. Peel the carrots and onions, and cut the carrots into thin slices, the onions into rings. Wash the celery and cut into ½-inch pieces. Melt the fat in a saucepan and add the carrots, onions, and celery; stew for about 5 mins. Add the stock (or water), salt and savory to taste and cook until soft. Add the strained beans, heat up and serve with chopped parsley.

Bubble and Squeak (Cabbage, Potatoes, and Onions). For 4

1 medium cabbage	2 medium onions
¾–1 lb. potatoes	3 oz. fat

Wash the cabbage and shred it coarsely. Wash the potatoes and cook them in their skins. Peel and chop the onions. Melt half the fat in a saucepan, add the cabbage (no water) and stew over a low heat for 10 to 15 mins. Peel the potatoes and cut them into ½-inch slices. Heat the remaining fat in a frying pan and fry the onion for a few minutes, then add the potatoes, and continue frying until they are very light brown. Finally mix everything together, add a little salt and serve at once.

NOTE. This is a meal in itself and a good way to use left-over potatoes.

Vegetable Chop Suey. For 4

½ head celery	3 Tbs. oil
½ small cabbage	4 Tbs. water
2 large onions	½ tsp. yeast extract
(or leeks)	½ tsp. soya sauce
2 large carrots	1½–2 Tbs. cornflour
¼ lb. bean sprouts	1 cup stock
(or 1 small tin)	salt to taste

After washing or peeling, slice the carrots and onions and cut the celery and cabbage into 1-inch pieces. Heat the oil in a saucepan, add the vegetables, stir in order to cover the vegetables with the oil, and stew for 3 to 5 mins. Add the stock, bring back to the boil, and stew for another 3 to 5 mins. over low heat, then add the yeast extract and the soya sauce. Blend the cornflour with the water, add to the vegetables and cook for another 3 to 5 mins. The bean sprouts can either be added to the vegetables at the last minute, or cooked separately in boiling water for a minute and then added. Serve with boiled rice (page 123).

NOTE. The cooking time of 3 to 5 mins. between the various stages is only a rough guide. Chop Suey is easily over-cooked; it is therefore better to err on the 'underdone' side.

Dolmades (Savoy Cabbage, Mushrooms, and Scrambled Egg). For 4

1 medium savoy cabbage	½ tsp. flour
¼ lb. mushrooms	3 Tbs. milk
1 small onion	1 oz. grated cheese
3 eggs	1 oz. breadcrumbs
2 oz. fat	salt to taste

Take the large outside leaves from the cabbage and wash them very carefully. Cook them together with the rest of the cabbage for a short time; they should be not quite soft. Take out of the water, keep the large leaves separate and chop the rest of the cabbage finely. Whisk the eggs together with the milk, the flour, and a little salt, and scramble the eggs in the usual way, using ½ oz. of the fat. Fry the onions and mushrooms together in another ½ oz. of the fat. Now grease a fireproof dish and cover the bottom with some of the large cabbage leaves. Put in a layer of scrambled egg, then a layer of chopped cabbage, then a layer of mushroom plus onions and repeat this layering until all vegetables are used up. Cover with some more of the large cabbage leaves. Sprinkle with the grated cheese and breadcrumbs and put the remaining fat in little dabs on top. Bake in a moderate oven (350–400°, Reg. 4–5) for about 30 mins. or until the top is golden brown. Serve with Gravy (page 96) or Tomato Sauce (page 101).

Goulash Bulgarian Style. For 4

2 small peppers	2 oz. oil
1 aubergine*	1 clove garlic
2 large onions	½ pt stock or water
1 lb. potatoes	a little cayenne pepper
½ lb. tomatoes	chopped parsley

After washing and preparing the vegetables cut the potatoes, onions, aubergines, and tomatoes into thick slices, the peppers in small strips. Stew the onions and peppers in the oil for 5 mins., add the aubergines and the finely chopped garlic and stew for another 5 minutes. Add salt to taste, a little cayenne

*Half a small marrow can be used instead.

pepper, the potatoes and tomatoes; stew for another 5 mins.
and only now add the stock or water. Stew slowly for another
15 to 20 mins. or until the potatoes are soft but not mashy.
Serve with chopped parsley.

Goulash Hungarian Style. For 4

2 small peppers	2 oz. oil
1 aubergine*	1 clove garlic
2 large onions	1 bayleaf
½ lb. tomatoes	½ pt stock or water
4 oz. rice	a little cayenne pepper
chopped parsley	

Prepare and stew the vegetables exactly as in the previous recipe.
After putting in the tomatoes add the rice and stew gently for
another 5 to 10 mins., stirring from time to time to prevent
sticking. Add the bayleaf and stock (or water). Cook over a low
heat until all the stock is absorbed and the rice is soft but the
individual rice grains still whole. Serve with chopped parsley.

Irish Stew. For 4

1 small green cabbage	2 medium onions
2 medium carrots	2 oz. fat
1 turnip or ½ swede	½ pt stock or water
2 leeks	½ tsp. yeast extract
1 large tomato	salt to taste
2 large potatoes	

Peel the carrots, turnip, and potatoes and cut them into ¼-inch
slices. Wash the cabbage and quarter or cut it coarsely. Peel the
onions and cut them into rings. The leeks are washed and cut
across into 2-inch pieces. Melt the fat in a saucepan and add the
root vegetables (except the potatoes) and stew for 5 mins., then
add the onions, leeks, and cabbage, and stew for another 5 mins.
Then add the potatoes and lastly the quartered tomato. Add the
stock (or water), the bayleaf and cook over low heat for 30 to 40
mins. or until the vegetables are soft but not mashy. Lastly mix
in the yeast extract, salt if desired, and remove the bayleaf. Very
tasty with Dumplings (pages 158–9).

* Half a small marrow can be used instead.

Leipziger Allerlei (Mixed Vegetable Dish). For 4

1 small celeriac	1 small cauliflower
2 large or 4 small carrots	4 large or 8 small sticks asparagus
1 small turnip	½ tsp. yeast extract
½ lb. garden peas	Cream Sauce (page 95)

Other vegetables may be used, but no onions or leeks and nothing which would make the dish mashy (potatoes, tomatoes).

After peeling cut all the root vegetables into ¼-inch cubes. It is advisable to cook the vegetables separately; if this cannot be done, start with the carrots, cook for 5 mins. and then add the other two vegetables. The peas must be cooked separately. So must the cauliflower, after it has been washed thoroughly and the little sprigs separated; the stalks can be cut into ¼-inch cubes and added. The asparagus is also cooked separately (see page 45) and kept hot in its cooking water. All the vegetables are strained, and the cooking water can then be used for making the cream sauce. Mix the yeast extract into the sauce and then all the vegetables except the asparagus. The cauliflower should be added last as the cooked sprigs break easily and all vegetables should remain whole and recognizable in the finished dish. Heat up and top with the asparagus and, if desired, some chopped parsley.

NOTE. The original Leipziger Allerlei should have one or two truffles added, but the dish tastes just as nice without.

Ratatouille Niçoise. For 4

1 large or 2 small peppers	1 clove garlic
2 medium aubergines	1 bayleaf
2 baby marrows	2 oz. oil
3 medium onions	salt or garlic salt
3 large tomatoes	chopped parsley

Prepare the vegetables in the usual way (if in doubt, refer to individual recipes) and cut the peppers in thin strips, the onions into fairly thick slices, and the aubergines and marrows into 1-inch cubes; the garlic is chopped finely. Heat the oil in a saucepan, add the garlic, onions, and peppers and stew for 5 mins. then add the aubergines and marrow cubes and stew for another 5 to 10 mins. on a moderate heat. Add the halved tomatoes and the bayleaf. Cook for another 5 mins. or a little longer if the vegetables are not quite soft; but do not overcook. Remove the bayleaf, add a little salt to taste, and serve with chopped parsley.

PULSE DISHES (FROM DRIED PEAS, BEANS, AND LENTILS)

The following dishes can be used instead of fresh vegetables when these are scarce, or they can be part of the main course served together with some fresh vegetables, since they are rich in protein.

NOTE. All dried pulses need soaking, preferably overnight, in enough water to allow them to swell. A good sized pot should be used and the water level should be as deep again as the dried pulses.

Dried Beans

These are available in various sizes and colours, but all taste very nearly the same. In the following recipes the ordinary dried white beans (haricot beans) are used but other kinds can be substituted.

Baked Beans in Tomato Sauce. For 4

1 lb. white beans	½ oz. fat
½ pt Tomato Sauce (page 101)	1 bayleaf

Soak the beans (see note above) and cook them in the soaking water with the bayleaf for 1 hour. Melt the fat in a fireproof dish and pour the beans, which need not be soft at this stage, together with the cooking water into the dish. Bake for about 2 hours in a moderate oven (350°, Reg. 5). Make a tomato sauce, pour it over the beans and heat up again in the oven.

Baked Beans with Parsley Sauce. For 4

1 lb. white beans	½ oz. fat
½ pt Parsley Sauce (page 101)	1 bayleaf

Exactly as in the previous recipe but with Parsley Sauce instead of Tomato Sauce.

Haricot Beans with Tomatoes. For 4

½ lb. white beans	1 oz. fat
1 medium onion	1 clove garlic
½ lb. tomatoes	chopped parsley

Soak the beans and cook them until soft. Chop up the onion and cut the tomatoes in half. Heat the fat in a saucepan, add the onion and tomatoes, and fry 5 mins. Add the chopped garlic, mix the beans into the saucepan, heat up and serve with chopped parsley.

Haricot Beans with Barley. For 4

6 oz. white beans	1½ oz. fat
1½ oz. pearl barley	chopped parsley
2 medium onions	salt to taste

Soak the beans and cook until soft, then strain them. Wash the barley, boil it until quite soft, then strain it. Heat ½ oz. fat in a frying pan and fry the onions until light brown. Now mix all three items, beans, barley, and onion, together, heat up again and serve with chopped parsley.

Haricot Stew. For 4

½ lb. white beans	½ stick celery
1 large carrot	1 oz. fat
2 large potatoes	marjoram to taste
1 medium onion	chopped parsley
2 medium leeks	salt to taste

Soak the beans and cook them in the same water until they are soft. Prepare the vegetables, the carrots, potatoes, and onions cut in cubes, the leeks and celery in ½-inch pieces, and stew in ½ oz. fat until not quite soft. Add them to the beans and cook together until the vegetables are quite soft. There should be very little of the water left by now. Mix in the remaining fat, marjoram and salt to taste, heat up again and serve with chopped parsley.

Lentils

There are two main kinds available. The best known are the

Egyptian ones, yellow-red and small, and the larger brown ones, grown chiefly in Poland and Russia.

Lentil Pudding. For 4

1 lb. lentils (red or brown)	1 oz. fat
½ lb. potatoes	1 bayleaf
1 large onion	salt to taste

Soak the lentils and cook until very soft. Strain and mash them. Make mashed potatoes (page 111) and mix with the mashed lentils, adding a little of the water in which the lentils were cooked. Fry the chopped onions in the fat until golden brown and empty the frying pan (onions and fat) into the lentil-potato mixture. Mix and add salt to taste. Put in a pudding bowl and steam in a water bath for an hour. Hot fried pieces of bread go well with this dish.

Lentil Pie. For 4

12 oz. lentils	1 oz. fat
½ lb. potatoes	1 bayleaf

Soak, cook, and mash the lentils as in the previous recipe. Add the bayleaf. Make mashed potatoes (page 111) out of the ½ lb. potatoes. Grease a fireproof dish, put in the mashed lentils, cover with the mashed potatoes and make a grooved pattern on top, criss-crossing with a fork (to let the fat run into the grooves). Cut the remaining fat into small pieces and put them on top. Bake in a moderate oven (350°, Reg. 5) for 30 mins.

Brown Lentil Stew. For 4

½ lb. brown lentils*	1½ oz. fat
1 medium carrot	1 oz. flour
2 leeks	¼ pt stock or water
½ stick celery	chopped parsley
1 large onion	salt to taste

Soak and cook the lentils until soft; only a little water should be left. If more is left, drain off the surplus. Prepare and stew the vegetables as in Haricot Stew (page 91), mix with the lentils and

* Red lentils are not suitable.

cook until the vegetables are soft, stirring from time to time to prevent sticking. Melt the fat in a saucepan, add the flour, stew for 2 to 3 mins. and add the stock (or water, perhaps from the drained-off surplus), stirring all the time. Then mix everything together, add salt to taste, heat up, and serve with chopped parsley.

Dried Peas

There are the whole green and the split green ones, and the split yellow peas. Any one kind can be used for the following recipes.

Pease Pudding. For 4

½ lb. dried peas	1 large onion
½ lb. potatoes	1 oz. fat

The method is exactly as given for Lentil Pudding (page 92).

Dhal. For 4

1 lb. yellow split peas	2 oz. fat
2 medium onions	½ tsp. cummin or fennel seeds*
1 or 2 chillies*	

Soak the peas and cook as explained in the introduction (page 90). Chop the onions and chillies and fry in 1 oz. fat until well browned. Add this to the cooked peas. Melt the rest of the fat in a frying pan and put in the cummin or fennel seeds and, as soon as the seeds start popping, pour the fat and seeds over the cooked pea-onion mixture. Put in a fireproof dish and bake in a slow oven for 20 to 30 mins.

Kedgeree. For 4

12 oz. split peas or lentils	1½ oz. fat
6 oz. rice	½ tsp. cummin or fennel seeds*

* If neither of the seeds are available 2 tsp. curry powder may be used.
For the Dhal add another ½ tsp. curry powder if no chillies are available either; or fry a medium onion in the fat until brown and mix into the peas or lentils and rice.

Wash and soak the peas and cook in the soaking water until nearly, but not quite, soft. Wash the rice and add it to the peas. Cook it until it is quite soft, but with the rice grains still whole. Melt the fat in a frying pan and put the cummin or fennel seeds into it and, as soon as the seeds start popping, pour the fat and seeds over the cooked rice and pea mixture and mix everything together.

Hot sauces for vegetables

In many cases sauces form an integral part of cooked vegetables to improve their taste or their nutritive value, but some of them are good enough to be served as a separate item with potatoes, rice, spaghetti, etc.

If you are ever stuck because you want a good sauce for a particular dish, consult the list on pages 102 f.

Cold sauces are described in the section for Uncooked Dishes and Salads (pages 169 ff.).

Cream Sauce or White Sauce. For 4

This is a basic recipe, the most frequently referred to.

1 oz. fat or butter	Optional:
2 oz. plain flour	salt
1 cup milk	nutmeg
½ cup stock or water	yeast extract

Melt the fat in a saucepan and add the flour. Stew for 2 to 3 mins. blending the ingredients well with a whisk or wooden spoon. Add the stock (or water) and the milk which may be cold or warm. Cook for 5 to 10 mins., stir or whisk quite briskly at first until you are sure there are no lumps, then stir gently to prevent sticking.

The above quantities are for a fairly thick sauce. More liquid will thin it to any consistency required.

This, so far, is the basic recipe. For most vegetables it is recommended you should season it a little with salt and a very little nutmeg and yeast extract.

Asparagus Sauce. For 4

½ lb. fresh asparagus or	½ oz. butter
a small tin	a few drops of lemon juice
Cream Sauce (previous recipe)	

Prepare and cook the asparagus as on page 45. The cooking water (or the water from the asparagus tin) should be used for making the cream sauce. Cut the asparagus into small pieces, using only the soft part. Make the cream sauce as in the previous recipe, preferably with butter, season it and add the asparagus pieces, the extra ½ oz. butter and the lemon juice. Heat up and serve.

Béchamel Sauce. For 4

1 small onion	Cream Sauce (see above)
½ oz. fat	

Make the cream sauce, fry the onion, and add it to the cream sauce.

Brown Butter Sauce. For 4

3 oz. fresh butter

Heat the butter until it turns light brown. It must be served in a very hot dish, preferably with a lid, as the butter will congeal as it cools.

Brown Sauce (Vegetarian Gravy). For 4

1 oz. fat or butter	1 small onion
2 oz. plain flour	2 tsp. yeast extract
1 cup milk	1 bayleaf
½ cup stock or water	salt to taste

Melt the fat in a saucepan and add the chopped onion. Fry until the onion is light brown, add the flour, and stew until the blended mixture shows a brownish colour (about 5 to 7 mins.) stirring continuously. Add the stock (or water), the milk, and the bayleaf and cook for another 10 to 15 mins., stirring from time to time and mixing in the yeast extract and salt during the last few minutes. It can be thinned by adding more milk, stock, or water.

Bordelaise Sauce. For 6

2 oz. mushrooms (cooked)	1½ oz. fat or butter
2 oz. asparagus (cooked)	1 pt milk
2 oz. peas (cooked or frozen)	2 oz. flour
1 small onion	nutmeg and salt to taste

Make a cream sauce (page 95) with 1 oz. fat (preferably butter), the milk, and the flour. Melt the rest of the fat in a frying pan, add the chopped onion and fry lightly, without browning. Mix the contents of the frying pan into the cream sauce, also the chopped mushrooms, the asparagus pieces and peas, add salt and nutmeg and cook for another 5 mins., stirring all the time.

Cheese Sauce. For 4

Cream Sauce (page 95)
2 oz. grated cheese

Make a cream sauce, season it, and mix in the grated cheese. The sauce should not boil when the cheese is mixed in as some cheeses get rubbery when heated up too much.

Curry Sauce. For 6

2 oz. fat	1 tsp. brown sugar
2 oz. flour	2 Tbs. curry powder
1 pt stock or water	grated rind and juice of a
2 medium onions	small lemon
2 medium cooking apples	1 or 2 bayleaves
½ oz. raisins	a little salt

Heat up the stock (or water) with the bayleaf, sugar, and salt; boil for 10 mins. Peel and chop the onions and apples, and chop the raisins too. Now melt the fat in a saucepan, add the flour and curry powder, and stew for a few minutes, stirring all the time. Add the stock (which may be hot but not boiling) and cook slowly for about 5 mins., again stirring all the time. Then mix in all the other ingredients and cook for another 10 mins. If you want a smooth sauce, you can strain it, but it will taste stronger if it is not strained but rather cooked a little longer so that all the ingredients are soft and mashy.

Egg Sauce. For 4

Cream Sauce (page 95)	1 tsp. lemon juice
2 hard-boiled eggs	chopped parsley

Make the cream sauce, season without the nutmeg. Chop the eggs finely, and add them to the sauce, as well as the lemon juice and the chopped parsley. Mix in and serve.

Fennel Sauce. For 4

Cream Sauce (page 95)
1 Tbs. lemon juice
grated rind of lemon
2–3 tsp. sugar

0 Tbs. chopped fennel
1 egg yolk
2 Tbs. cream or top of milk

Make the cream sauce; add lemon juice, rind, fennel, and sugar. Then take a slightly warmed mixing bowl, put in the cream (or milk) and egg yolk, mix, and then pour the hot cream sauce in very carefully and slowly, whisking all the time.

Fricassée Sauce. For 4

Egg Sauce (as above)
1 tsp. chopped capers
2 tsp. chopped pickled
gherkins

½ tsp. chopped fresh tarragon
1 small chopped
fresh spring onion

Make the egg sauce (page 97) and mix all the other ingredients into it.

Gravy. See Brown Sauce (page 96).

Herb Sauce. For 4

finely chopped fresh herbs such as:
parsley, chervil, tarragon, marjoram,
summer savory, and, if desired, 2
small fresh spring onions.

Cream Sauce (page 95)

Make the cream sauce and mix the herbs into it.

Hollandaise Sauce (1) Very rich. For 4 to 6

4 oz. butter
2 egg yolks
1 Tbs. lemon juice
½ bayleaf

1 sprig fresh tarragon
1 clove (optional)
2–3 Tbs. water
a little salt

This sauce is somewhat like a hot mayonnaise and should have the same consistency when finished. First boil the tarragon, bayleaf, and clove (optional) in 2 to 3 Tbs. water; keep boiling. As the sauce itself must never boil, a double saucepan is required.

Start over a low heat with 1½ oz. butter, the egg yolks, and the lemon juice, stirring with a whisk all the time – in fact, whisking should never stop until the sauce is finished. When the butter is completely dissolved and blended in with the egg yolks add the rest of the butter in two or three stages as the mixture gets thicker. Finally add the boiling water in which the tarragon etc. was cooked and which has been strained. Stir over a low heat for another minute and serve at once.

Hollandaise Sauce (2) Less rich. For 4

2 Tbs. butter	1 sprig tarragon
3 Tbs. flour	1 egg yolk
2 cups stock or water	1 Tbs. cream or milk
a little salt	1 Tbs. lemon juice

Heat 1 Tbs. butter in a saucepan, add the flour and stew for a few minutes, then add the stock (or water) and cook for another 5 mins., add the tarragon, the salt, and the rest of the butter, stirring all the time until the butter is dissolved. Take off the flame and add the lemon juice. Then, carefully, add the egg yolk which had been mixed with the cream, stirring all the time to prevent the egg from curdling. Another method for the last stage is to mix the egg yolk with the cream in a mixing bowl and add to it the hot sauce taken from the flame, starting slowly and stirring all the time.

Horseradish Sauce. For 4

1½ oz. fat	1 pt stock or water
1½ oz. flour	4 Tbs. vinegar
2 tsp. mustard powder	3 oz. grated fresh horseradish
1 tsp. sugar	

Melt the fat in a saucepan, add the flour and mustard powder, stew for 2 to 3 mins., stirring all the time. Add the stock (or water) and cook for another 5 mins., stirring from time to time. Stir in the sugar, a little salt, and the vinegar, take off the flame and add the grated horseradish.

This sauce can also be served cold.

Mousseline Sauce. For 4

This may also be considered as a third type of Hollandaise Sauce.

3 Tbs. water	1 Tbs. cornflour or
1 Tbs. lemon juice	arrowroot
1 sprig tarragon	2 egg yolks
1 small onion	2 oz. butter
½ bayleaf	2 oz. rich cream
½ cup stock (or water)	salt to taste

Make a herb extract by boiling 3 Tbs. water with the lemon juice, onion, tarragon, and bayleaf until it is reduced by half, then strain and keep for later. Blend the cornflower or arrowroot with the cold stock (or water) and bring to the boil, stirring all the time. Now in a double saucepan, over boiling water, whisk the egg yolks with the herb extract until the mixture thickens. Remove it from the flame and add the butter in small pieces to the mixture gradually, stirring all the time; then add the cornflour mixture, still stirring. Finally whip the cream stiffly and add it carefully to the sauce.

This sauce can also be served cold.

Mushroom Sauce. For 4

Cream Sauce (page 95)	2 medium onions
1 oz. fat	1 bayleaf
4 oz. mushrooms	salt to taste

Wash and chop the mushrooms and the peeled onions. Stew the onions in the fat for about 2 mins., then add the mushrooms and stew for another 5 to 6 mins. Make a cream sauce and mix everything together, including the bayleaf. Cook slowly for another 5 mins.

Mustard Sauce. For 4

Cream Sauce (page 95)	½ bayleaf
4 tsp. mustard powder	2 peppercorns
1 Tbs. vinegar	salt to taste
½ lemon	

Make a cream sauce, mixing the dry mustard powder with the

flour. Then add all the other ingredients and cook for another 5 to 10 mins.

Onion Sauce. For 4

2 or 3 medium onions
1½ oz. fat

Brown Sauce (page 96)

Chop the onions and fry in the fat until golden brown. Make the brown sauce and mix together.

Parsley Sauce. For 4

Cream Sauce (page 95)
Chopped fresh parsley

Make a cream sauce and add the chopped parsley.

Pimento or Capsicum Sauce. For 4

1 oz. fat
1 oz. flour
1 medium pepper
1 medium onion

2 cups stock or water
2 Tbs. cream or top of milk
salt to taste

Fry the chopped onions and chopped pepper together in the fat for a few minutes, then add the flour, stew for another 2 mins., add the stock (or water), and cook over a gentle heat for about 20 mins., stirring from time to time. Take off the flame and add the cream just before serving.

Piquant Sauce. For 4

Pimento Sauce (previous recipe)
1 gherkin
2 olives

1 medium tomato
1 tsp. capers
a little lemon juice

Make the pimento sauce, then add the finely chopped tomato, gherkin, olives, and capers, and finally a few drops of lemon juice. Other seasonings, if desired, to taste.

Tomato Sauce (1). For 4

Cream Sauce (page 95)
1 small onion

½ oz. fat
½ small tin of tomato purée

Make the cream sauce but season only with a little garlic salt

(no nutmeg, no yeast extract). Fry the chopped onion in the fat,
add this and the tomato purée to the cream sauce, heat up and
serve.

Tomato Sauce (2). For 4

1 lb. ripe tomatoes*	1 small clove garlic
1 medium onion	a little thyme
3 Tbs. oil	salt and pepper to taste

Wash the tomatoes in hot water and peel them; chop the onions
finely. Fry the onions slightly in the oil (they must still be white),
add the tomatoes, salt, pepper, thyme, and garlic (or garlic salt).
Boil vigorously until the tomatoes are quite soft and the quantity
of the sauce reduced to about half. This will take up to an hour
and the result should be a thick sauce. No water should be used
and no attempt should be made to thicken the sauce with flour.

Table of Sauces and Their Uses

THIS SAUCE	GOES WELL WITH
Asparagus Sauce	salsify, seakale.
Béchamel Sauce	broad beans, runner beans, French beans; all green vegetables such as cabbage, spinach, broccoli, sprouts; root vegetables such as carrots, parsnips, turnips, swedes but not with beetroots; also with mushrooms.
Brown Butter Sauce	asparagus, French beans, broccoli, cauliflower, chicory, corn, peas, salsify, seakale, samphire.
Brown Sauce (Vegetarian Gravy)	most of the Main Course Dishes (page 116), especially pastry dishes. Also with broad beans, green cabbage, chicory, celery, onions.
Bordelaise Sauce	purple broccoli, salsify, seakale, celeriac.
Cheese Sauce	all 'au gratin' vegetables; further with Jerusalem artichokes, broccoli, sprouts, green cabbage, celery, mixed greens, leeks, lettuce, marrow, onions, parsnips, salsify, spinach, tomatoes, turnips and tops, celeriac.
Curry Sauce	mixed vegetables, cooked rice, cauliflower, marrow, hard-boiled egg.
Egg Sauce	asparagus, mushrooms, seakale, salsify, carrots, marrow.

* Tinned whole tomatoes can be used instead.

THIS SAUCE	GOES WELL WITH
Fennel Sauce	carrots, marrow, parsnips.
Fricassée Sauce	semolina dishes, boiled rice, boiled macaroni and spaghetti, Jerusalem artichokes, marrow, seakale.
Herb Sauce	Jerusalem artichokes, celery, marrow, parsnips, salsify, turnips, kohlrabi.
Hollandaise Sauce	asparagus, globe and Jerusalem artichokes, cauliflower, marrow, seakale, salsify.
Horseradish Sauce	beetroot, parsnips, salsify, marrow, vegetable rissole, nut roast.
Mousseline Sauce	asparagus, globe artichokes, celery, marrow, celeriac, salsify, seakale.
Mushroom Sauce	broad beans, sprouts, celery, marrow, seakale, spinach, aubergines; also with most Main Course Dishes (page 116), especially those made with pastry and rice.
Mustard Sauce	marrow, seakale, boiled rice, Bavarian dumplings, Swiss vegetable dumplings.
Onion Sauce	broad beans, broccoli, green cabbage, mixed greens, kale, parsnips, salsify, turnips, swedes, spinach; most Main Course Dishes (page 116), especially pastry dishes.
Parsley Sauce	Jerusalem artichokes, broad beans, runner beans, carrots, cauliflower, celery, marrow, parsnips, seakale, celeriac.
Pimento Sauce	celery, marrow, parsnips, swedes, turnips; dumplings, noodles, macaroni, spaghetti.
Piquant Sauce	celery, marrow, parsnips, swedes, turnips, celeriac, kohlrabi; semolina dishes except those made with cheese.
Tomato Sauce (1)	runner beans, sprouts, cauliflower, celery, marrow, pepper, seakale, salsify, turnips, aubergines, celeriac, fennel; most Main Course Dishes (page 116), especially those made with macaroni, spaghetti, rice, and semolina.
Rich Tomato Sauce (2)	This is *the* sauce for macaroni and spaghetti; also useful with rice and semolina, some pastry dishes such as Cornish Pasty, Baked Savoury Roll, and vegetables such as cauliflower, marrow, pepper, salsify.

Potato dishes

Whenever possible potatoes should be cooked in their skins as valuable minerals get lost if they are peeled in their raw state. A pressure cooker is very useful for boiling potatoes.

The following recipes are not in alphabetical order but rather begin with the more simple dishes and become gradually more elaborate.

BAKED

Baked Potatoes. For 4

4 large potatoes
a little oil

Scrub the potatoes thoroughly and cut a cross on top of each. Then paint them with a little oil, put them into a hot oven (450°, Reg. 7 or 8), straight on the shelves, and bake them for about 45 mins., or until they are soft (squeezing them a little to test this). Then take them out, open up the cross on top by pressing the sides slightly. A piece of butter or cheese can be placed in this opening.

Bircher Potatoes. For 4

8 medium potatoes   1 tsp. salt
1 Tbs. oil   1 tsp. caraway seeds

Scrub the potatoes thoroughly, as the skin is meant to be eaten too. Cut each potato in half and paint thickly with oil. Put them on an oiled baking sheet with the cut face down. Sprinkle the salt over the potato tops, then the caraway seeds. Bake in a moderate oven (350°, Reg. 5) for about 40 to 50 mins.

Roast Potatoes. For 4

8 medium potatoes
2 oz. fat

Wash and peel the potatoes and cut them in half. Heat the fat in a fireproof dish in a hot oven (400–450°, Reg. 6–8), put the potatoes in and roast them for about 20 mins., then turn them and roast for another 20 mins. or until they are brown outside and soft inside. Use no water.

Stuffed Baked Potatoes. For 4

4 large potatoes	1 oz. fat
1 pt stock or water	salt to taste
Stuffing	
½ oz. fat	1 oz. cooked mushrooms
2 oz. breadcrumbs	1 egg
1 oz. grated nuts	marjoram and salt to taste
1 small onion	

Cook the peeled potatoes until they are half done. Then cut them in half and scoop out a small part with a teaspoon or – better – a vegetable scoop.

Peel and chop the onion and fry in ½ oz. fat until light brown. Mix the breadcrumbs and grated nuts together, add the onion and the cooked chopped mushrooms. Add salt and marjoram to taste. Mix in the beaten egg. If the mixture is very stiff, add a little milk or cream. Divide the mixture into 8 portions and stuff the potatoes. Now pour the stock (or water) into a fireproof dish and place the potatoes side by side in it. Dab each potato with a little fat and bake in a moderate oven (350°, Reg. 5) for about 20 to 30 mins., or until the potatoes are soft and slightly brown.

FRIED

Fried Potatoes (1). For 4

1½ lb. potatoes	salt to taste
½ cup oil	chopped parsley

Wash, peel, and cut the potatoes into thin slices. Heat the oil in a frying pan until fairly hot, then add the potato slices and sprinkle a little salt on top. Cover with a lid and fry over a low flame for 5 to 7 mins. Turn the potatoes, replace the lid, and fry for another 5 to 7 mins., until the potatoes are soft. They need not be brown. Sprinkle with chopped parsley and serve.

Prepared in this way they taste quite different from ordinary sauté potatoes (see next recipe).

Fried Potatoes (2) (Pommes Sautées). For 4

Made from cooked or left-over potatoes.

1½ lb. cooked potatoes	a little salt
3 Tbs. oil	1 onion (optional)

Cut the cooked potatoes into slices, not so thin that they break, or into ½-inch cubes. Heat the oil in a frying pan, and fry the potatoes until they start to brown. Add a little salt and, if wanted, add the chopped onion now. Turn and continue frying until the potatoes (and onion) are well browned. The onion must not be added too soon as it will brown more quickly than the potatoes.

Potatoes Lyonnaise. For 4

1½ lb. cooked potatoes	3 oz. fat
½ lb. onions	salt to taste

Peel the onion and cut it into slices. Fry them in a frying pan with 1 oz. fat until they turn a very light yellow. Take off the flame and keep separate. Then fry the cooked and sliced potatoes in the rest of the fat until slightly brown. Put one layer of these potatoes in a fireproof dish, then a layer of the onions, repeat, and finish with a layer of potatoes. There is probably enough fat still round the onions and potatoes but a few pieces of fat or butter can also be placed on top. Bake in moderate oven (350°, Reg. 5) for about 20 mins.

Cheese Potatoes. For 4

1 lb. cooked potatoes	3 Tbs. oil
1½ oz. grated cheese	chopped parsley

Proceed exactly as for Fried Potatoes (2), but without adding any onion. When finished, take off the flame and stir in the grated cheese. Serve with chopped parsley.

Swiss Potato Rösti. For 4

1½ lb. cooked potatoes
3 Tbs. oil

This is a good way of using left-over potatoes, as the potatoes should be cooked the day before anyhow.

Cut them into thin slices or grate them coarsely. Melt the fat in a frying pan, add the potatoes and sprinkle a little salt over them. Cover with a lid and fry over a low flame until they are light brown, turning them occasionally. When they are nearly done, form them into a flat cake-shape by pressing the potatoes from the top and the sides with two knives or palette knives. Fry the cake for another few minutes so that a brown crust forms underneath. Finally, turn the cake over on to the serving plate with the crust on top, taking care not to spoil the shape.

Bauernfrühstück (Farmer's Breakfast). For 4

1 lb. cooked potatoes	3 Tbs. oil
3 eggs	¼ cup milk
2 slices bread	1 tsp. flour
1 large onion	chopped parsley

Cut the potatoes into large (½-inch) cubes, the bread into very small ones. Chop the onion and fry in ½ Tbs. oil until light brown. Put it in a bowl to cool. Fry the bread cubes in another ½ Tbs. oil, also until light brown, then add them to the onion. Heat the remaining 2 Tbs. oil in a frying pan and fry the potatoes as for Fried Potatoes (2) (page 106). Meanwhile break the eggs into a mixing bowl, add the flour, milk, and a little salt, and whisk thoroughly. When the potatoes are almost ready add the bread cubes and onions to heat up and pour the egg mixture over th whole, stirring or turning from time to time until the egg is set. Serve in a hot dish topped with chopped parsley.

Potato Cakes. For 4

1 lb. potatoes
1 or 2 eggs
2 oz. flour
2–3 oz. fat

1 small onion (optional)
seasoning to taste,
i.e. marjoram, thyme, parsley,
    nutmeg, and salt

Left-over potatoes can be used. Otherwise boil the potatoes, floury ones preferably, and strain. Mash thoroughly, cool a little, and add the flour and egg. Chop the onion, if wanted, and the herbs very finely and stir into the mixture together with nutmeg and salt. Let the mixture cool completely, then mould it between your hands into flat round cakes, about 3 inches across. It will not stick to your hands if you dip them first in some flour. Fry the cakes in the fat on both sides to a golden brown.

They can be served cold, but taste better hot.

Pommes Provençale (Garlic Potatoes). For 4

1½ lb. cooked potatoes
3 Tbs. oil

1 onion
1 clove garlic

Exactly as Fried Potatoes (2) (page 106), but with chopped garlic added with the salt.

Potato Griddle Cakes. For 4

Made from raw potatoes, these are extremely popular in Germany where they are known as *Kartoffelpuffer* or, in the western parts, as *Reibekuchen*. They are sold hot in the streets in parts of Berlin and the Rhineland.

1 lb. potatoes
1 medium onion
2 Tbs. flour
a little salt

oil for frying, the amount
depending on the type of
potatoes

Peel the potatoes and onion. Grate both on a medium grater. The mixture should be moist. If it is too watery, press out the surplus water. Add the flour and salt. If the potatoes are very floury, use less than the 2 Tbs. flour. Fill the frying pan ¼ full with oil and heat up. Put 1 Tbs. of the mixture into the frying pan, pressing it down with a fork to form a thin (¼-inch) cake. Do this with as many as the frying pan will take. Fry on a moderate flame until the undersides are light brown. Then turn them over with a palette knive and fry the other sides. Keep hot and serve in a very hot dish. If the griddle cakes are brown outside and still raw inside, reduce the flame a little.

FRIED IN DEEP FAT

Chipped Potatoes. For 4

1½ lb. potatoes	a little salt
1 pt oil	1 clove garlic (optional)

Wash and peel the potatoes and cut them into chips. Dry them with a towel and keep them in the towel until they are used, to prevent them from discolouring. Heat the oil in a heavy saucepan which is big enough – the pint of oil should not do more than half-fill it. Heat the oil to 370° (or just *before* it gives off blue smoke). Then drop in a few chips at a time to prevent the oil from cooling down too much. After 4 to 6 mins. the chips will still be pale and not quite ready. This is the time to take them out with a perforated spoon or wire ladle and put them on a plate with some blotting paper. This completes the first stage. Before serving, heat the oil again and fry the chips for another minute or two until they are hot and golden brown. Take out and serve on a hot plate covered with blotting paper. Usually a little salt is sprinkled over them, and some finely chopped garlic can be mixed with the salt.

This method may sound a little cumbersome but all others produce soggy, greasy chips.

Potato Crisps. For 4

1½ lb. potatoes	a little salt
1 pt oil	1 clove garlic (optional)

After they have been washed and peeled the potatoes should be cut into very thin slices (see also next recipe). Put them into the hot oil and take them out as soon as they get brown. Drain and sprinkle a little salt over them. If wanted, the finely chopped garlic can be mixed with the salt.

Potato Wafers. For 4

A special vegetable slicer (colloquially called a mandoline) is needed for this, the wavy knife edge being used.

Quantities and method as previous recipe but the slices are cut by the wavy knife, the potato being turned 90° after each cut.

Parisian Potatoes (Pommes Noisette). For 4

1½ lb. large potatoes
1 pt oil

Wash and peel the potatoes. With a vegetable scoop cut out little balls (the size of a hazelnut or slightly larger), dry them on a towel, and proceed as for Chipped Potatoes (page 109).

Potato Beignets. For 4

4–6 large cooked potatoes
1 pt oil
a little salt

For beignet batter
4 oz. S.R. flour
1 egg
¼ pt milk

Left-over potatoes can be used. Cut the potatoes into thick slices so that they do not break. Make a batter of the flour, egg, and milk by mixing the three ingredients together in a bowl. Heat the oil until very hot (but not smoking), dip one potato slice at a time into the batter, coat them well and drop them gently into the hot oil. Fry them in two or three batches (you would require more oil if they were all to be fried together) until golden brown. Lift out with a wire ladle, drain, and put on a very hot dish for serving. A little salt may be sprinkled on top.

Potato Croquettes. For 4

1½ lb. cooked potatoes
1 Tbs. milk
1 Tbs. flour
2 eggs

1 pt oil
breadcrumbs
nutmeg and salt to taste

Mash the potatoes and mix with the milk, flour, and 1 egg. Add nutmeg and salt to taste. Form into small croquettes (about 2½ inches long). Beat the other egg, coat the croquettes with it, and roll them in breadcrumbs. Fry in deep fat until golden brown.

OTHER POTATO DISHES

Mashed Potatoes. For 4

1½ lb. potatoes
2 Tbs. hot milk
or water

1½ oz. butter or fat
salt and nutmeg to taste
chopped parsley

Wash and peel the potatoes and cut them into pieces of roughly equal size. Cook until soft, strain, and mash them with a potato masher or by pressing them through a sieve. (The potatoes can also be cooked in their jackets and should then be peeled when hot and mashed immediately.) Put potatoes back into the saucepan and heat over low flame together with the butter (or fat) and hot milk (or hot potato water), stirring all the time to prevent burning. Then beat them with a strong wire whisk to make them light and fluffy. Serve with chopped parsley.

Potato Snow. For 4

1½ lb. potatoes
2 oz. butter (optional)

Peel and cut the potatoes as in the previous recipe. Only floury potatoes are suitable. Cook them until soft, strain well, and press them through a potato press or a strong colander straight on the serving dish. Heat the butter (optional) and pour over the snow.

Potato Soufflé. For 4

1½ lb. potatoes
2 oz. butter or fat
2 Tbs. milk or water

3 eggs
breadcrumbs
salt and nutmeg

Prepare and boil the potatoes as for Mashed Potatoes (above). Put them through a press or mash; they should be quite dry. Separate the egg yolks and mix them, together with the butter, milk (or potato water), salt, and nutmeg, into the potatoes. Whip the egg whites stiffly and fold gently into the mixture. Grease a fireproof dish and sprinkle with breadcrumbs. Put the potato mixture into it and bake in moderate oven (350°, Reg. 5) for 30 to 35 mins.

Potato Pudding. For 4

1½ lb. potatoes	¼ tsp. marjoram
2 eggs	a little salt
2 oz. butter or fat	nutmeg to taste

Make a mixture of these ingredients by the same method as in previous recipe. Then pile the mixture into a greased pudding bowl and steam in a water bath for an hour.

Italian Potatoes. For 4

1½ lb. potatoes	½ cup of milk or
2 eggs	potato water
2 oz. grated cheese	2 Tbs. breadcrumbs
2 oz. butter or fat	salt and nutmeg to taste

Prepare and boil the potatoes as for Mashed Potatoes (page 111). Mix with the milk (or potato water) and eggs together with about three quarters of the butter and cheese. Grease a fireproof dish, put the mixture into it and top with breadcrumbs, the rest of the butter, and the cheese, and bake in moderate oven (350°, Reg. 5) for 30 to 40 mins. until the top is brown.

Potato Dumplings. For 4

1½ lb. potatoes	*Optional*
6 oz. cornflour	2 slices bread
1 cup water	1 oz. fat

Left-over potatoes can be used. Grate finely. If the potatoes are freshly cooked let them cool for ½ hour before grating. Mix with the cornflour. Then bring a cup of water to the boil, pour it over the mixture, and add salt to taste. Mix everything well with a whisk, then form dumplings and boil them slowly in a large saucepan in boiling salt water for about 10 mins. Simmer for another 10 mins. and serve.

Optional and to make the dish more interesting: make croûtons by cutting the bread into small cubes and frying them in fat until golden brown. When forming the dumplings put a few croûtons in the middle. The cooking time is the same.

NOTE. This dish goes well with Red Cabbage (page 51) or just served with Horseradish Sauce (page 99).

Duchess Potatoes. For 4

1½ lb. cooked potatoes
2 egg yolks
2 Tbs. milk

2 oz. butter or fat
salt and nutmeg to taste

First mash the potatoes (left-overs can be used), then heat the milk and dissolve the butter (or fat) in it. Mix well with the potatoes, egg yolks, salt, and nutmeg. Put the mixture in a forcing bag with a large star and pipe rosettes on to a greased baking sheet. Some pressure has to be used as the mixture is fairly stiff. Bake in hot oven (425–450°, Reg. 6–7) until brown.

Parsley Potatoes. For 4

1½ lb. potatoes
2 oz. butter or fat

1½ Tbs. chopped parsley
salt to taste

Wash and peel the potatoes, quarter them and boil until soft but not mashy. Strain. Melt the butter (or fat) in a saucepan, add the chopped parsley and the potatoes. Then shake the saucepan to distribute the parsley evenly over the potatoes.

Herb Potatoes. For 4

1½ lb. potatoes
1 small onion
2 oz. fat
½ pt stock or water

herbs such as:
parsley, chervil, marjoram,
thyme, tarragon, etc.

Wash the potatoes, and peel and cut them into thick slices. Chop the onion; the herbs can be chopped up together. Stew the onion in the fat for 2 to 3 mins., then add the potatoes and stew for another 2 to 3 mins., stirring from time to time. Add the stock (or water), salt to taste (very little), and cook for about 20 mins., or until the potatoes are soft. Add the chopped herbs, shaking the saucepan to distribute them evenly.

Swiss Potatoes. For 4

1½ lb. potatoes
2 oz. fat

½ pt stock or water
2 tsp. yeast extract

Wash, peel, and quarter the potatoes. Melt the fat in a saucepan and add the potatoes. Stew for 2 to 3 mins., then add the stock (or water) and cook for another 20 mins. or until they are soft. Add the yeast extract, mix in well and cook for another minute. The water should by now be completely absorbed.

Carrot Potatoes. For 4

1 lb. potatoes	1 pt stock or water
½ lb. carrots	½ tsp. yeast extract
2 oz. fat	chopped parsley
1 small onion	salt to taste

Wash and peel the potatoes and carrots; cut them into 1-inch cubes. Peel and chop the onion. Melt the fat in a saucepan and fry the onion for 2 mins., add the carrots and stew for 5 mins., then add the potatoes and stew for another 5 mins. Neither the carrots nor the potatoes should get brown. Heat the stock or water with the yeast extract, add salt if desired, and pour over the carrot-potato mixture. Boil until the mixture is soft and nearly all the water is absorbed. Serve with chopped parsley.

Potato Ragoût. For 4

1½ lb. cooked potatoes	1 cooked carrot
2 oz. fat	a little cooked celery
2 oz. flour	(if available)
¾ pt milk or water	2 or 3 cooked mushrooms
1 tsp. capers	1 tsp. lemon juice or
2 small gherkins	vinegar
1 small bayleaf	

Left-over potatoes can be used, preferably cooked in their jackets. Peel and cut them into 1-inch cubes. Melt the fat in a saucepan, add the flour, blend well and stew for a few minutes. Add the milk or water and the bayleaf, cook slowly for 10 to 15 mins., stirring all the time. Remove the bayleaf. Cut the carrot, mushrooms, and celery into very small cubes, chop the gherkins and capers, add these ingredients to the sauce, and simmer for 5 mins. Then add the potatoes and heat up. Just before serving add the lemon juice or vinegar.

Princess Potatoes. For 4

1½ lb. potatoes	2 eggs
1 oz. grated cheese	1 tsp. flour
2 oz. fat	a little salt and nutmeg to taste
½ pt milk	

Wash the potatoes and boil them in their skins. Peel and cut them into thick slices. Grease a fireproof dish and put the sliced potatoes in in layers, sprinkling grated cheese between layers. Heat half the milk and half the fat and pour them over the potatoes. Bake in a hot oven for 10 to 20 mins. Now whisk together the eggs, flour, salt and nutmeg, and the rest of the milk. Pour this over the potatoes and dot little pieces of the rest of the fat on top. Return to the oven for another 15 mins. or until the mixture is set.

Sailor Potatoes. For 4 to 6

1 lb. potatoes	6 Vegetable Rissoles (page 136)
4 oz. fat or oil	2 tsp. flour
1 egg	salt to taste
½ cup milk	

Wash and peel the potatoes, and cut them into thin slices. Heat 3 oz. fat or oil in a frying pan and fry the raw potatoes very slowly, covering the pan with a lid. The potatoes need not be brown but should be soft. Cut the vegetable rissoles into slices or cubes (don't mash them), and put into a greased fireproof dish alternate layers of potatoes and pieces of rissole, ending with a layer of potatoes. Whisk the egg, milk, and flour together and pour over the potatoes. Finally put the rest of the fat in small pieces on top. Bake in a moderate oven (350°, Reg. 5) until the potatoes are brown on top and the egg-milk mixture has set, which will take about half an hour or a little longer.

This is almost a meal in itself, and goes well with salads.

Main course dishes

The dishes described in this chapter are in the widest sense the meat substitutes, providing some or all the protein for a healthy diet. Vegetarians call them 'savouries'. They are grouped somewhat arbitrarily because there are no clear-cut borderlines. A cheese soufflé for instance can be classified as an egg dish (as we have done) or as a cheese dish. In fact, many of the vegetable recipes to be found in the vegetable section, for instance the gratins and the pulse dishes, could be considered as main course dishes since they are fairly substantial.

We hope that this selection of 134 dishes proves that there is plenty of variety in a vegetarian diet.

How many vegetables should be served to make up the main course? This depends on individual tastes and on the type of savoury. At least one vegetable or salad should be served with any of them. If it contains in itself many vegetables, as does a vegetable pie, a side dish of potatoes or a salad may be sufficient. On the other hand, a plain omelette or a lentil rissole requires two vegetables, one of them perhaps a potato dish. A look at the Menu Suggestions (page 225) may give further indications.

STUFFED VEGETABLES

Cabbage Roulade. For 4

1 small Savoy or white cabbage	½ pt stock or water
1 oz. fat or butter	1 small onion
Stuffing	
4 oz. bread	1 oz. grated cheese
1½ cup milk	½ tsp. marjoram and tarragon
½ onion	1 egg
2 oz. mushrooms	a little garlic salt or garlic
1 oz. fat or butter	

Wash the cabbage and cook it for about 5 mins. Strain and let it cool. (During this time prepare the stuffing, see below.) Remove the leaves one by one; the large ones can be used as they are, one for each roulade, the smaller ones – two, three, or four together – to give enough coverage for each roulade. Spread the leaves on the table and put 1–2 Tbs. stuffing for each roulade on the leaves. Then roll them up lengthwise, and place them side by side in a greased fireproof dish. Fry the chopped onion in the fat until golden brown, spread it over the cabbage rolls, lastly pour the stock over them and bake in a moderate oven (350°, Reg. 6) for about 45 mins. to an hour.

For the stuffing cut the bread into large pieces and soak them in the milk for about ½ hour. Then put them through a mincer or mash with a fork. Wash and chop the mushrooms, peel and chop the onion, and fry both together in the fat. Then mix all the ingredients – the egg last – together. This stuffing should be fairly stiff. Breadcrumbs can be added if it is too soft.

Stuffed Globe Artichokes. For 4

4 large artichokes	2 oz. grated cheese
1 small onion	¾ pt stock or water
4 oz. rice	2 oz. butter or fat

In order to have a cup-shaped artichoke for stuffing, trim off the stem at the bottom and the uppermost leaf-tops (this is best done with a pair of scissors); then the artichokes are cooked as on page 74. Strain and cool. Then take out the inside leaves and remove carefully the hairy 'choke', leaving the artichoke bottom intact and the outer leaves standing. The artichokes are now ready for stuffing.

Wash the rice, peel and chop the onion. Melt 1½ oz. fat and fry the onion in a saucepan lightly. Then add the rice and stew for another 5 mins., stirring from time to time. Heat up the stock or water and pour it over the rice, adding a little salt. Boil gently until the rice is soft; the water or stock should by now have been completely absorbed by the rice. Now fill the artichokes with the cooked rice mixture, top thickly with the grated cheese and the rest of the butter. Place in a fireproof dish in which a little stock or water has been heated, and bake in hot oven (400°, Reg. 7) until the cheese is brown. A slice of tomato may be added on top as a garnish.

Stuffed Aubergines. For 4

2 aubergines	2 oz. oil
1 medium onion	3 Tbs. breadcrumbs or
2 large tomatoes	oatflakes
1 oz. grated nuts	1 clove garlic or
1 oz. grated cheese	garlic salt
Tomato Sauce (page 101)	salt to taste

Wash the aubergines and put them for about 5 mins. in boiling water (less time if they are young as they should not become soft at this stage). Cut them lengthwise in half and scoop out the inside, pips and all. When doing this take care not to damage the skin which will be used later. Peel the onion and cut it, together with the tomatoes, in small cubes. Heat the oil in a saucepan, add the finely chopped garlic (or garlic salt), then the onion, tomatoes, and chopped-up aubergines. Stew for about 5 mins. Add the breadcrumbs or oatflakes and the nuts, and mix well. Now fill the aubergine skins with the mixture, place them on a greased baking sheet, sprinkle the grated cheese on top, and bake in a moderate oven (350°, Reg. 5–6) for about 30 mins. or until the top is well browned. Serve with tomato sauce.

Stuffed Vegetable Marrow. For 4

1 medium marrow	¼ pt milk
2 oz. fat or butter	1 egg
2 oz. grated nuts	½ tsp. yeast extract
3 oz. breadcrumbs	1 oz. grated cheese
1 small onion	mixed herbs and salt to taste

Wash and scrub the marrow but do not peel it. Cut it lengthwise in half and scoop out the seeds and pith. If the marrow is young these can be used: chop them finely and fry them later with the onion. For the stuffing, mix the nuts, breadcrumbs, milk, herbs, and egg. Fry the chopped onion in a saucepan, then add the stuffing mixture and yeast extract and fry for another minute.

Boil the marrow for about 5 mins. and strain (it will still be fairly hard). Grease a fireproof dish and put in the marrow halves side by side, fill them with the stuffing mixture and top with small pieces of the remaining fat and the grated cheese. Bake in a moderate oven (350°, Reg. 5) for about 30 mins. To make serving easier you can cut the marrow into portions before baking. Serve with Brown Sauce (page 96) or Tomato Sauce (page 101).

Stuffed Onions. For 4

4 large onions	1 oz. breadcrumbs
1 oz. fat or butter	½ tsp. yeast extract
1 oz. grated nuts	marjoram and salt to taste

Peel the onions, take a slice off the top, and scoop out the centre to make room for 2–3 tsp. stuffing. Boil the onions for 15 mins. until not quite soft. For the stuffing, chop the scooped-out onion bits and fry them in a little fat. Mix them together with the nuts, breadcrumbs, yeast extract, and herbs. If the mixture is too stiff, add a little stock, milk, or water. Stuff the onions, top with the remainder of the fat, and bake in a greased fireproof dish in a moderate oven (350°, Reg. 5) for 20 to 30 mins. See that the onions stand upright in the dish.

Stuffed Tomatoes. For 4

4 large tomatoes	2 oz. cheese grated
2 oz. breadcrumbs	1 clove garlic or garlic salt
1 medium onion	chopped parsley and chives
1½ oz. fat or butter	

Wash the tomatoes, remove a slice from the top and scoop out the seeds and core. Chop these finely. Fry the chopped onion in ½ oz. fat until golden brown, then mix into it the chopped tomato seeds and core, the breadcrumbs, parsley, chives, and grated cheese. Fill the tomato cases with this mixture and put the slice from the top back again. Bake in a greased fireproof dish in a hot oven (400°, Reg. 6) for 10 to 15 mins.

A slight variation on this recipe is to cut the tomatoes in half, then proceed as above using only 1½ oz. grated cheese when preparing the stuffing. Top the stuffed tomatoes before baking with the remainder of the grated cheese.

Stuffed Turnips. For 4

4 turnips	½ pt stock or water
1 oz. grated cheese	
Stuffing	
2 oz. bread	½ oz. grated cheese
¾ cup milk	herbs (marjoram, thyme,
½ onion	and/or tarragon)
1 oz. mushrooms	1 small egg
½ oz. fat	garlic or garlic salt

Prepare the stuffing as described for Cabbage Roulade (page 116), but only from the quantities given above. Peel the turnips and scoop them out with a spoon or vegetable scoop to make room for 1 to 1½ Tbs. of filling in each turnip. Grease a casserole (including the lid), place the stuffed turnips in it, add the stock, and top with grated cheese. Cover the casserole tightly and bake in a hot oven (425°, Reg. 7) for 40 to 50 mins.; the cheese topping should be brown when done.

Stuffed Kohlrabi. For 4

See page 78.

Stuffed Green Peppers. For 4

4 large peppers	¾ pt stock or water
1 small onion	a clove of garlic or
4 oz. rice	garlic salt
2 oz. fat	Tomato Sauce (page 101)

Wash the peppers and cut off the tops, which will be used later as lids. Remove all the seeds and discard them. Prepare the stuffing as for Stuffed Globe Artichokes (page 117) without the cheese and with the addition of the garlic, or garlic salt instead of ordinary salt. Also prepare tomato sauce. After the rice stuffing is cooked, divide it into four portions, stuff the peppers, and replace the tops. Grease a fireproof dish and put the peppers in it. Add ½ cup of stock or water and place a piece of greaseproof paper on top. Bake in a moderate oven (350°, Reg. 5) for half an hour. Then remove the paper and pour half the tomato sauce over the peppers, and bake for another 15 mins. Heat up the rest of the sauce and serve it separately with the peppers.

Tomato Egg Farci. For 4

4 large tomatoes	½ oz. fat
2 eggs	2 Tbs. milk or cream
½ oz. flour	salt to taste

Cut a slice off the top of the tomato and scoop out most of the inside. Beat the eggs together with the milk, flour, chopped scooped-out tomato, and salt. Pour this mixture into the tomato cases. Grease a fireproof dish with ½ oz. fat and bake the tomatoes in it for about 20 mins. in a hot oven (400°, Reg. 6).

Stuffed Cabbage Dish. For 4

This is a dish consisting of alternate layers of cabbage and stuffing.

1 medium savoy cabbage	1 small onion
2 oz. fat or butter	salt to taste
Stuffing	
3 oz. rice	1 oz. grated cheese
½ oz. fat	2 oz. mushrooms
1 egg	1 small onion
2 cups stock	mixed herbs

Cut the washed cabbage in fairly large strips. Melt 1½ oz. fat in a large frying pan, add the chopped onion and the cabbage, and fry for about 10 mins., stirring from time to time. Then take off the flame but keep warm. For the stuffing, wash the rice, strain it, and cook it in 2 cups of stock or water until soft. Fry the mushrooms and onions in ½ oz. fat and mix this with the rice, cheese, herbs, and egg. Then grease a fireproof dish and fill it with alternate layers of the cabbage mixture and stuffing, finishing with a layer of cabbage. The remaining fat or butter is put in small pieces on top. Bake in a fairly hot oven (375–400°, Reg. 6 or 7) for about 30 mins. Very tasty with Tomato Sauce (page 101) or a salad.

RICE DISHES

Risotto. For 4

½ lb. rice	½ pt stock or water
2 oz. fat	1 tsp. yeast extract
1 onion	chopped parsley
1 carrot	salt to taste
a few pieces of celery	1 Tbs. grated cheese (optional)

Peel the onion and carrot and cut them and the celery into small
cubes. Melt the fat in a saucepan and stew the vegetables for
about 5 mins. Wash the rice in cold water, strain it, and add it to
the vegetables. Stew over a gentle heat until the rice begins to
look transparent. In the meantime heat up the stock or water
together with the yeast extract, then pour it over the rice. Cook
for another 15 to 20 mins.; the rice will then be soft but not
mashy. Top with chopped parsley and – optional – with grated
cheese, and serve at once.

Mushroom Rice. For 4

Exactly as previous recipe, but use 4 oz. of mushrooms instead
of the other vegetables.

Spanish Rice. For 4

Again as Risotto (above), but replace the carrot and celery with
1 or 2 leeks and a small green pepper.

Pilaff (Turkish Rice). For 4

½ lb. rice	½ lb. tomatoes
1½ oz. fat	1 onion
1 pt stock or water	salt to taste

Melt 1 oz. fat in a saucepan, add the washed and rinsed rice,
and cook it for 5 mins. (by which time the rice should have
become translucent). Then add the heated stock or water and
boil for 15 to 20 mins.; the liquid should by then be absorbed
and the rice dry and soft. Cut the onions into thin slices, the
tomatoes in half. Fry the onions until light yellow, add the
tomatoes and stew together for 5 to 7 mins. Mix this carefully
with the rice and serve.

Spinach Rice. For 4

½ lb. rice
2 oz. fat
½ lb. spinach
1 onion

¾ pt stock or water
1 tsp. yeast extract
chopped parsley
1 Tbs. grated cheese (optional)

Prepare a Risotto (page 122), but with ½ lb. chopped raw spinach instead of the other vegetables. The quantity of stock (or water) should be reduced as spinach is rather watery in itself.

Rice Croquettes. For 4

½ lb. rice
¾ pt stock or water
1 leek or 1 onion
1½ oz. grated cheese

2 Tbs. flour
1 egg and a little milk
breadcrumbs
oil for frying

Cook the rice as in the risotto recipe (page 122) together with the leek or onion. Let it cool and mix with the flour and grated cheese. Form the mixture into croquettes about 3 inches long. Beat the egg and milk together, dip the croquettes into this and roll them in breadcrumbs, covering them well. Fry either in a large frying pan with plenty of oil or in deep fat.

Baked Tomato Rice. For 4

½ lb. rice
1 pt water

1 oz. fat
½ pt Tomato Sauce (page 101)

Cook the rice as for Plain Rice (next recipe). Grease a casserole dish and its lid. Rinse the cooked rice in cold water and put it in the casserole. Pour the tomato sauce over it and mix gently with the rice. Dab the fat in small pieces on top, cover and bake in a moderate hot oven (375°, Reg. 5) for about 1 or 1¼ hours.

Plain Rice. For 4

½ lb. rice
1 pt water

Boil the rice in the water until the water is absorbed (about 15 mins.). An easier way to cook rice is in a double saucepan. Yet another way is to put the rice and the water in a covered casserole in the oven, though this takes longer.

SEMOLINA DISHES

Semolina Pudding with Grated Cheese. For 4

4 oz. semolina	½ oz. butter
1¼ pt milk*	2 oz. grated cheese
¾ pt water*	½ tsp. yeast extract

Bring the water (and milk) to the boil, add the yeast extract and pour in the dry semolina, stirring all the time. Cook for about 15 to 20 mins. Melt the butter and pour over the semolina, then top with grated cheese and serve.

Savoury Semolina Cakes. For 4

4 oz. semolina	½ tsp. yeast extract
1½ pt milk and water	1 egg
oil for frying	salt to taste

Bring the milk and water to the boil, and add yeast extract and salt if desired. Pour in the dry semolina, stirring all the time, and cook for about 15 to 20 mins. Spread the cooked semolina on a flat dish or board just under 1 inch thick and let it cool. Cut out little cakes with a 2-inch or 2½-inch round cutter. Beat the egg and dip the cakes into it. Fry them on both sides until light brown.

Semolina Gnocchi. For 4

4 oz. semolina	1 cup milk
1½ pt milk and water	1 oz. grated cheese
(or water only)	½ oz. butter
2 eggs	salt and nutmeg to taste

Cook the semolina as in the previous recipe, the salt and nutmeg, if desired, to go in before boiling the water. Put the cooked semolina in a flat dish (or dishes) so that it is about ½ inch deep. Let it get completely cold. Then cut it into small (1-inch) squares or use a 1 inch pastry cutter. Place these squares in a fireproof dish until it is well filled. Beat the eggs with the milk and pour over the gnocchis. Top with grated cheese and little dabs of butter. Bake in a moderate oven (350°, Reg. 5) for 30 to 45 mins.

* 2 pt water if milk is not used.

Fried Semolina Gnocchi. For 4

4 oz. semolina	salt and nutmeg to taste
1½ pt milk and water	oil for frying
(or water only)	

Cook and prepare gnocchi as in previous recipe but instead of baking them, fry them until light brown.

FARINACEOUS DISHES (PASTA)

Spaghetti Napolitana (with Tomato Sauce and Cheese). For 4

6 oz. spaghetti	½ pt Tomato Sauce (page 101)
½ oz. fat	2 oz. cheese (Parmesan or
a little salt	Cheddar)

Bring about 3 pt water (with a little salt if desired) to the boil. Add the spaghetti. If the genuine long spaghetti are used put them slowly into the boiling water. They will get soft immediately and coil themselves into the pan without breaking. Cook for not longer than 15 mins., perhaps rather less; over-cooking makes them sticky. Strain and pour cold water over the spaghetti. Then heat the fat in a saucepan and re-heat the spaghetti in it over a gentle flame. When hot put into a serving dish and pour the hot tomato sauce over it. Mixing the sauce into the spaghetti is usually done at the table. Serve the grated cheese separately.

Macaroni Napolitana. For 4

Exactly the same as in the previous recipe. The macaroni are usually broken into the boiling water.

Macaroni au Gratin. For 4

6 oz. macaroni	1 oz. grated cheese
½ pt Cheese Sauce (page 97)	nutmeg and salt to taste
½ oz. fat or butter	

Cook the macaroni as in the previous recipe. Strain and let some cold water run over it. Mix the cooked macaroni with the cheese sauce, add nutmeg and salt if desired, and put the mixture into a greased fireproof dish. Top with the grated cheese and little

dabs of fat or butter. Bake in a moderate oven (350°, Reg. 5) for
40 to 45 mins.; the top of the gratin should by then be quite
brown.

Spaghetti au Gratin. For 4

The same as in the preceding recipe. Use 6 oz. broken spaghetti.

Macaroni Lyonnaise. For 4

6 oz. macaroni cooked as for Macaroni Napolitana	2 medium onions 3 oz. fat

Peel and cut the onions into slices. Fry them lightly in 1 oz. fat.
Then melt the rest of the fat in a good-sized frying pan, add the
cooked macaroni and fry until they are just beginning to brown.
Add the onions and fry together until macaroni and onions are
well brown. Serve at once.

Macaroni (or Spaghetti) Stew. For 4

6 oz. cooked macaroni or spaghetti*	1 large potato
1 carrot	2 oz. fat
1 small leek	½ pt stock or water
1 onion	1 tsp. yeast extract
	parsley and/or chives

Peel and dice the carrot and potato. Cut the leek lengthwise in
half, wash it, and cut it into small pieces. Peel and chop the onion.
Melt 1 oz. fat in a saucepan and fry all the vegetables for a few
minutes, then add the stock (or water) and cook them until they
are soft. Add the cooked macaroni (or spaghetti), the yeast
extract, salt if desired, and the rest of the fat and heat up again.
Serve with chopped parsley and/or chives.

Spanish Egg Spaghetti. For 4

6 oz. cooked spaghetti*	2 Tbs. milk
1 medium green pepper	2 oz. fat
1 medium onion	salt to taste
2 eggs	

* Left-over spaghetti or macaroni can be used, otherwise cook from 3 oz.
dry macaroni or spaghetti.

Cut the pepper in half and remove all the seeds and pith. Cut into very small squares. Peel and chop the onion. Melt 1 oz. fat in a saucepan and stew the onion and pepper until soft, then add the remaining fat and the cooked spaghetti. Beat the eggs, milk, and salt together, pour it over the spaghetti mixture and stir until the eggs are set.

Macaroni Rissoles. For 4

4 oz. macaroni	1 oz. fat
1 oz. flour	2 eggs
1 onion	½ cup milk
1 tsp. chopped marjoram	3 Tbs. breadcrumbs
salt to taste	oil for deep frying

Cook the macaroni as for Macaroni Napolitana but do not pour cold water over it as the cooked macaroni should this time be rather sticky. Mix them with the flour. Chop and fry the onion in 1 oz. fat, add it with the marjoram and one egg to the macaroni, and mix well. Form rissoles about 3 inches long. If the mixture does not stick together, add more flour. Beat one egg with the milk, dip the rissoles into it, and cover them with breadcrumbs. Fry in deep fat until golden brown.

Home-made Noodles

Although good plain noodles can be bought ready for cooking, here is a recipe for home-made ones. The quantities given here will make 5–5½ oz.

4 oz. flour	½ Tbs. oil
1 large egg	salt optional
1 Tbs. water	

Sift the flour on to a board or table. Make a well in the centre and put in all the other ingredients. Mix to a dough. If it is mixed properly no bubbles should appear when it is cut through. Let it stand for 30 mins. Divide the dough in two and roll out each piece as thinly as possible, as thin as paper even. Keep the pieces separate and let them dry for an hour. Then roll up each piece and cut them into very fine strips with a sharp knife. Loosen them carefully from time to time. Put them on a cloth to dry again. These noodles should not be kept for too long as they contain no chemical preservative.

Noodle Tomato Pudding. For 4

6 oz. noodles	Tomato Sauce (page 101)
2 oz. grated cheese	1 oz. fat

Cook the noodles in 2 pt boiling water until they are soft, then strain and pour cold water over them. Put them into a greased fireproof dish, top with the grated cheese and the tomato sauce. Finally dab the fat in small pieces on top. Bake in a moderate oven (350°, Reg. 5) for 30 to 40 mins.

Ravioli. For 4

5½ oz. flour	1 Tbs. water
1 Tbs. oil	1 oz. grated cheese
1 egg	salt optional

Mix the sifted flour with the oil, water, and salt to a smooth paste, and let it stand for 15 to 20 mins. Divide the mixture into two pieces and roll it out as thinly as possible. Leave for an hour. Then spread one piece on the table and place small heaps of filling (see next recipe) with a tsp. or piping bag on it. (There should be enough space between the heaps to allow the upper layer to be stuck on the lower one.) Then cover it with the other piece, pressing it down on the lower layer in the spaces between the heaps of filling. Cut out the squares with a knife or pastry wheel. Then drop the pieces, a few at a time, into a fairly large saucepan of boiling water and cook until they rise to the surface. Take them out with a perforated spoon or ladle and put them into a heated serving dish, sprinkling grated cheese between the layers of ravioli. This is usually served with melted butter, tomato sauce, or any other suitable hot sauce.

Filling for Ravioli. For 4 to 6

Any of the rice dishes (page 122) (left-overs) can be used if they are dry enough. Here is a recipe for spinach rice filling:

3 oz. rice	2–3 Tbs. grated cheese
6–8 oz. cooked spinach	

Cook the rice as for Risotto (page 122). Mix well with the chopped spinach and grated cheese.

PANCAKE AND OTHER BATTER SAVOURIES

Pancakes, although usually considered as sweets, can easily be adapted to make excellent main course dishes. Use a thin batter, in contrast to batter puddings. It should be well beaten in order to get plenty of air into the mixture and to make the pancake light and fluffy. Thick batters should be beaten just enough to make a smooth mixture, as too much beating will make the pudding rather leathery.

Basic Pancake Recipe. For 4 (2 pancakes each)

4 oz. flour
1 egg
salt optional

½ pt milk (perhaps more or less according to type of flour used)

Sift the flour (and salt if desired) into a mixing bowl, make a well in the middle, and put the egg and half the milk into it. Start mixing from the centre working in the flour gradually from the sides. Beat thoroughly, adding the rest of the milk after some time. For frying use a small frying pan preferably; otherwise only part of a larger one. Distribute a little oil evenly in the pan and heat. When hot pour a little batter into it, using a large spoon or ladle, and distribute it evenly over the surface by tilting the pan from side to side. Fry for not more than two minutes until the underside is slightly brown, shaking the pan a little to stop the pancake sticking, and using the palette knife to loosen the edges. Then turn the pancake over and fry the other side, which takes even less time as the mixture is now hot.

As the pancakes are done, keep them hot, preferably on blotting or greaseproof paper, until all the pancakes are fried and ready for filling.

Filled Savoury Pancakes. For 4

Many vegetables and vegetable dishes (left-overs, for instance) can be used for filling savoury pancakes. The filling should be hot. Use ½ Tbs. for each pancake. Keep the pancakes in a hot oven until they are all filled.

Tomato and Onion Filling. For 4

½ lb. tomatoes	1 oz. fat
2 medium onions	salt to taste

Slice the tomatoes and onions. Stew them together in the fat until soft.

Spanish Filling. For 4

1 green pepper	2 onions
2 tomatoes	1 oz. fat

Prepare the pepper as on page 79 and cut it into thin small slices. Slice the onions and tomatoes. Stew everything together in the fat until soft.

Aubergine Filling. For 4

1 aubergine	1 oz. fat
1 onion	garlic or garlic salt

Boil the aubergine for 5 mins. (it should not be soft at this stage), peel, and chop up the inside together with the onion. Add chopped garlic (or garlic salt) and fry in the fat until soft.

Cheese Pancake. For 4

Exactly as plain pancake (basic recipe page 129) but mix 1 oz. grated cheese into the pancake batter before frying.

Corn Pancake. For 4

Use basic pancake recipe (page 129) but mix 4 Tbs. corn off the cob into the pancake batter before frying.

Pancake aux Fines Herbes. For 4

Use basic pancake recipe (page 129) and mix chopped herbs (such as thyme, chervil, parsley, chives, savory) into the pancake batter before frying.

Spanish Pancakes. For 4

Prepare the Spanish filling as on page 131 and mix into the batter (prepared as on page 129) before frying the pancakes.

Spinach Pancake Dish. For 4 to 6

Pancakes made according to basic recipe (page 129) plus:	2 eggs
	1 oz. fat
1 lb. spinach	1 cup milk
1 medium onion	1 Tbs. flour

Wash the spinach and chop coarsely. Melt the fat in a saucepan, add the chopped onion and fry until light brown, then add the spinach and cook over low flame until tender. Fill the pancakes with this mixture, about 1 Tbs. to each pancake, roll them up and place them side by side in a greased fireproof dish, which should not be more than three-quarters full. Whisk the eggs, milk, and flour together and pour over the pancakes. Bake in a moderate oven (375°, Reg. 6) for 20 to 30 mins.

Soya Pancakes. For 4

4 oz. flour	2 cups water
2 Tbs. soya flour	1 tsp. oil
½ tsp. baking powder	salt to taste

Put the dry ingredients into a mixing bowl, add the water gradually, whisking all the time, then whisk in the oil. Let this mixture, which should be like cream, stand for 30 to 40 mins. After this it should be of the same consistency as the ordinary pancake mixture. If it is too thin, add more flour, if too thick more water. Then fry the pancakes as described on page 129.

Yorkshire Pudding. For 4

4 oz. flour	½ pt milk
1 egg	½–1 oz. fat

Make a batter mixture as described on page 129. Put the fat in a shallow fireproof dish and heat in a very hot oven (500°, Reg. 10) until the fat starts smoking. Then pour in the batter and cook

for 10 mins. Reduce the heat to 425°, Reg. 7, and cook for
another 25 mins., or until the pudding is brown and has risen
well.

Individual Yorkshire Puddings. For 4

The same as in the previous recipe, but the baking is done in
deep patty tins or small pudding bowls with a slightly shorter
baking time.

Toad-in-the-Hole. For 6

> ingredients as Yorkshire Pudding (page 131)
> plus 6 Mushroom Rissoles (page 136)

Melt 1 oz. fat in a fireproof dish and place the rissoles in it with
space for the batter between the rissoles. Heat in a very hot oven
(500°, Reg. 10) until the fat begins to smoke. Pour in the pudding
batter and proceed as for Yorkshire Pudding (page 131).

VEGETABLE BEIGNETS

These are often called fritters and consist of vegetables dipped
into a batter and then fried in deep fat to a golden brown. They
look very attractive as a main course with vegetables. It should
be noted, however, that they are not rich in protein. It is therefore
advisable to include in the menu items which provide some protein, such as for instance eggs, gratin dishes, and cheese sauces.

First, here are two batters, (1) with and (2) without egg.
They are both equally suitable for beignets.

Batter (1)

> 4 oz. plain flour
> 2 tsp. baking powder
> 1 egg
> ¼ pt milk
>
> 1 tsp. oil
> a little salt and perhaps a few
> grains of cayenne pepper

Mix the flour with the baking powder, then add egg, milk, oil,
and seasoning. Let the mixture stand for at least ½ hour before
being used.

Batter (2) (without egg)

4 oz. plain flour
2 tsp. baking powder
1 tsp. cream of tartar

¼ pt apple juice, milk, or water
1 tsp. oil
seasoning to taste

Mix the flour with the baking powder and cream of tartar, then add the apple juice (milk or water) whisking vigorously. Lastly add the oil slowly, still whisking all the time. Let it stand at least half an hour before being used.

Jerusalem Artichoke Beignets. For 4

4 large or 8 small
   artichokes

batter
fat or oil for frying

Prepare and cook the artichokes as for steamed on page 43. Cut them lengthwise into thick slices, dip them in batter, and fry them.

Beetroot Beignets. For 4

2 medium cooked beetroots
Batter (2)

oil for frying

Peel and cut the beetroots into thick slices. Dip them in batter, preferably No. 2 (because of the colour), and fry them.

Cauliflower Beignets. For 4

1 medium cauliflower (cooked)
batter

oil for frying

Divide the cauliflower into 4 or 8 sprigs, and dry them in a towel. Dip in batter and fry them.

Celeriac Beignets. For 4

1 medium celeriac
batter and oil

Scrub the celeriac and boil with the peel on until nearly soft. Then peel and cut it into slices about ½ inch thick. Dip them in batter and fry them.

Swede or Turnip Beignets. For 4

1½ lb. swedes or turnips   oil for frying
batter

Wash and peel the swedes or turnips. Cut away any woody parts
and boil them until nearly soft. Then cut them into slices, dip
them in batter, and fry them.

Apple Fritters (or Beignets). For 4

4 medium cooking apples   oil for frying
batter

Peel and core the whole apples and cut them into thick slices.
Dip them into the batter and fry until golden brown.

RISSOLES, ROASTS, AND CUTLETS

The 'nut cutlets' of music-hall fame belong here, but readers
will have realized by now that they form only a small part of the
vast array of vegetarian dishes. Rissoles and cutlets differ, of
course, only in their shape. Some people prefer these dishes to
be served in the shape of cutlets in order to emphasize that they
are meant as meat substitutes; others prefer not to be reminded
of this. We believe that these are excellent dishes in their own
right and describe them as 'rissoles'.

Lentil Rissole. For 4

¼ lb. red lentils   2 Tbs. milk
3 onions   marjoram and thyme
2 eggs   salt to taste
3 cups breadcrumbs   oil for frying

Soak the lentils overnight in 1½ pt water, then cook them in this
water until quite soft (when the water will probably have disappeared through absorption and evaporation). Mix the lentils
with 2 cups of breadcrumbs, 1 egg, salt, and herbs, then let
them stand for ½ hour. After this, form them into rissoles or any
other shape. Beat the egg and milk together, dip the rissoles
into it, and cover them with the rest of the breadcrumbs. Finally,
fry them in plenty of oil or even in deep fat until well browned.

Nut Rissole or Cutlet. For 4

2 oz. grated nuts*	2 Tbs. milk
4 oz. breadcrumbs	1 tsp. yeast extract
2 oz. fat	½ pt stock or water
2 oz. flour	marjoram and thyme
salt to taste	oil for frying
1 egg	

Melt the fat in a saucepan, add the flour and stew for two minutes. Then add the stock (or water), salt, herbs, and yeast extract, and cook for 5 to 10 mins., stirring all the time. Take off the flame, add 3 oz. of the breadcrumbs and the nuts. Cool and shape the mixture into rissoles or cutlets. Beat the egg and milk together, dip the rissoles into this and coat with the remainder of the breadcrumbs. Fry in plenty of oil or in deep fat until well browned.

Nut Roast (1). For 4   3 REALLY. DON'T OVERCOOK OR BISCUITY

Same ingredients as previous recipe with ½ oz. fat
   instead of the frying oil

Make the same mixture as in the previous recipe including in it the egg, milk, and all the breadcrumbs. When cold shape the mixture into a large square or two smaller ones, put it in a greased fireproof dish, and top with little dabs of fat. Bake in a moderate oven (375°, Reg. 5 to 6) for 30 to 40 mins. This dish can be served with Gravy (page 96) or Tomato Sauce (page 101).

Nut Roast (2). For 4

½ lb. grated nuts*	2 eggs
½ lb. tomatoes	1 tsp. chopped thyme and
1 small onion	marjoram
½ oz. fat	salt to taste

Skin and slice the tomatoes. Peel and chop the onion finely. Mix the nuts, tomatoes, and onions together with the well-beaten

* Any nuts (except peanuts which are not real nuts) can be used, but hazelnuts are best for this dish. Before being grated they should be slightly roasted in a slow oven (275°, Reg. 2) for ½ hour. After this, put them on a towel and rub off the brown skin, then grate or grind.

eggs. Add salt (if desired) and herbs. Grease a fireproof dish well, add the mixture and bake in a hot oven (400–425°, Reg. 7 or 8) for 30 to 40 mins. It should rise like a cake and will be golden brown when it is ready. Turn it out on a hot plate and serve hot with Gravy (page 96) or cold with salads.

Vegetable Rissole or Cutlet. For 4

1 leek*	3 oz. oat flakes
2 medium carrots*	1 Tbs. flour
1 turnip*	1 tsp. yeast extract
leaves of celery*	marjoram, thyme and/or
2 small onions	savory, 1 bayleaf
2 oz. fat	salt or garlic salt

The vegetables should be cut finely or grated on a fine grater. Melt the fat in a shallow saucepan (or deep frying pan) and fry the vegetables in it slowly until they are nearly – but not quite – soft. Add no water! Chop the herbs, including the bayleaf, together with one small onion very finely and add them to the vegetables just before they are taken off the flame. Then add the yeast extract and the salt or garlic salt. Put the mixture in a bowl and let it cool. Finally add the oat flakes, the flour and the other chopped raw onion, shape into rissoles, and fry in plenty of oil or in deep fat.

Mushroom Rissole. For 4

The same as in the previous recipe, but using $\frac{1}{2}$ lb. of sliced, fried mushrooms and 2 sliced and fried onions in place of the vegetables.

Egg and Cheese Rissole. For 4 to 6

4 hard-boiled eggs	$1\frac{1}{2}$ cup milk or water
1 small raw egg	$\frac{1}{2}$ oz. breadcrumbs
3 oz. grated cheese	$\frac{1}{2}$ tsp. mixed herbs
1 oz. fat	salt
1 oz. flour	$\frac{1}{2}$ tsp. mustard } optional
oil for frying	

* Other vegetables or a different combination may be used.

Shell the boiled eggs and cut into slices. Melt the fat in a saucepan, add the flour and stew for 2 mins.; add 1 cup milk (or water)
and stew for another 5 mins., stirring all the time. Add salt,
herbs, and mustard. Take off the flame and mix the cheese and
egg slices into it. When cool, shape the mixture into rissoles or
cutlets. Beat the raw egg and the rest of the milk together, dip
the rissoles into it, coat with breadcrumbs, and fry either in
deep fat or in a frying pan.

These rissoles are fairly rich and make a meal when served
with a sauce (Tomato Sauce, page 101, or Gravy, page 96) and a
simple salad.

EGG DISHES

Plain Omelette. For 1

2 eggs
1 Tbs. (level) fat or oil
(margarine or butter – unless clarified – are unsuitable, as they
brown too quickly)

The whole secret of making a perfect omelette is to have all
ingredients and tools (a very clean frying pan, a fork, and a
palette knife) handy in order to fry the omelette in one go without stopping; it should not take longer than a minute and a half.
You also need the right flame or heat: if it is too hot the omelette
will brown; too low it will be leathery. After one or two tries
every omelette will turn out perfectly.

Break the eggs into a basin and whisk well, preferably with a
fork as the mixture should not be foamy. Heat the fat in the
frying pan – until it is hot but not smoking – pour in the egg and
have the flame hot enough to cook the omelette quickly. The
underside will of course set first. Keep the liquid egg moving
by stirring with the round side of a fork so that it runs to the
hot part of the frying pan; or by lifting the set underside
slightly and tilting the pan so that the liquid runs underneath.
As soon as nearly all the egg is set take the pan off the flame, tilt
it, and roll the omelette over, away from the handle side, on to a

hot plate, helping it gently along with the fork or palette knife. Serve at once.

NOTE. If you are making filled omelettes, have the filling ready and hot so that the omelette does not have to wait for it.

Cheese Omelette. For 1

Make a plain omelette as above. Put 1 Tbs. grated cheese in the centre of the omelette before rolling it up. Top the finished omelette with some grated cheese.

Tomato Omelette. For 1

Have 1 large or 2 small stewed and chopped up tomatoes ready and put them on the omelette before it is rolled up.

Spinach Omelette. For 1

Fill an omelette with 1 slightly heaped Tbs. of cooked spinach before rolling it up.

Asparagus Omelette. For 1

Fill an omelette with 3 or 4 sticks of cooked asparagus, cut into small pieces before rolling it up. Decorate the finished omelette with two more sticks.

Mushroom Omelette. For 1

Fill an omelette with a slightly heaped Tbs. of fried mushrooms.

Omelette aux Fines Herbes. For 1

Make a plain omelette (page 137) but mix 1 Tbs. mixed chopped herbs (parsley, chives, chervil, rosemary, savory) into the egg mixture when whisking.

Filled Curry Omelette. For 1

Make a plain omelette (page 137) and add ½ tsp. curry powder to the egg mixture before frying. It can be filled with 1 Tbs. Risotto (page 122) or any other rice dish which may be at hand (left-over), for example those on page 123.

Indian Corn Omelette. For 1

As in the previous recipe, and filled with 2 Tbs. sweet corn off the cob. Tasty also without the curry powder.

Spanish Omelette. For 1

As plain omelette (page 137) with the following filling:

1 medium potato (cooked)	½ oz. fat
¼ green pepper	salt to taste
½ onion	

Melt the fat in a frying pan, add the chopped onion and pepper and fry until the onion begins to brown, add the potato – cut into small cubes - and fry for another few minutes until the potatoes are hot but not brown.

Chicory Egg Dish. For 4

½ lb. chicory	2 Tbs. milk
1 oz. fat	1 tsp. flour
4 eggs	salt to taste

Clean the chicory and cook it in water until fairly, but not quite, soft. Strain. Melt ¾ oz. fat in a frying pan and fry the chicory on both sides until light brown, then add the remaining fat. Whisk the eggs together with the milk and flour (and salt if desired) and pour the mixture over the chicory. As soon as the egg starts setting, turn the chicory over so that the liquid egg can run underneath. Repeat until all the egg is set. Serve at once.

Tomato Eggs. For 4

4 large tomatoes	4 eggs
1 large onion	2 Tbs. milk
1 oz. fat	1 tsp. flour

Fry the sliced onion in ¾ oz. fat until very light brown, then add the tomatoes, cut in half, and continue frying until the tomatoes are soft but not mashy. Then proceed as in previous recipe with the egg, milk, and flour mixture.

Mushroom Egg Dish. For 4

½ lb. mushrooms	4 eggs
1 large onion	2 Tbs. milk
1 oz. fat	1 tsp. flour

Fry the sliced onion in ¾ oz. fat for 2 mins., then add the quartered mushroom and continue frying for not more than 5 mins. The mushrooms should be slightly underdone. Then add the egg, milk, and flour mixture as for Chicory Egg Dish above and proceed in the same way.

Scotch Eggs. For 4

4 boiled eggs	½ cup milk
1 raw egg	1 oz. breadcrumbs
Nut Rissole mixture (page 135)	oil or fat for frying

The boiled eggs should be not quite hard (6 mins.) as the frying later will make them harder still. After preparing the nut rissole mixture, roll it out to a thickness of about ¼ to ½ inch and cut out squares large enough for each to cover one egg completely. Wrap the mixture round the shelled eggs and seal all the corners by pressing the mixture round the egg with your hands. Beat the raw egg and milk together, dip the whole eggs into it and coat them with breadcrumbs. Then fry in deep fat or oil until well browned. They look more attractive when cut in half just before being served.

Also useful as a cold savoury with salad.

Curried Egg and Rice. For 4

4 hard-boiled eggs	1 pt Curry Sauce (page 97)
½ lb. rice	

Cook the rice in boiling water (see also page 123) and keep it hot. Shell the eggs immediately they are boiled. Place the rice on a shallow dish and make a well in the centre (to take the sauce later). Cut the eggs in half, place them round the well and pour the curry sauce over it. See that all items, the dish, the rice, the eggs, and the sauce, are really hot.

Egg Fricassée. For 4

4 hard-boiled eggs	4 small gherkins
2 oz. fat	1 Tbs. capers
2 oz. flour	1 Tbs. vinegar
1½ pt stock or water	½ bayleaf
1 small onion	salt to taste

Melt 1 oz. fat in a saucepan, and fry the chopped onion for 2 mins., then add the remaining fat, heat it, add the flour, and stew everything for another 2 mins., stirring all the time. Add the stock or water (and salt if desired) and cook for another 5 mins., still stirring. Now add the chopped capers, gherkins, the bayleaf, and lastly the vinegar. Cook over a very low flame for another 5 mins. This is now the fricassée sauce. Shell the eggs and cut them in slices. Place them carefully in the sauce and serve.

A very attractive dish can be made when this egg fricassée is served on a shallow dish with Pommes Noisette (Parisian Potatoes, page 110) round it.

Cheese Soufflé. For 4

1½ oz. butter or margarine	½ tsp. yeast extract
3 oz. flour (white)	3–4 oz. grated cheese
1–1¼ pt milk	nutmeg and salt to taste
4 eggs	

Melt the butter in a saucepan, add the flour and stew over a low flame for 2 mins. Heat the milk, adding the salt, nutmeg, and yeast extract, pour it into the butter-flour mixture and cook for another 5 to 6 mins., stirring all the time. Take the pan off the flame and let it cool a little (so that the eggs which will be added next will not set). In the meantime beat the egg whites to a stiff froth. Add the egg yolks, one by one, to the cooled mixture. After this add the grated cheese (or if you make a different – say mushroom – soufflé, the mushrooms, etc.). Then carefully add the stiff egg white, folding it in with a metal spoon, and do not stir the mixture after this. Grease a soufflé dish or other fireproof dish which is large enough to allow the mixture to rise to double its height. Bake in a hot oven (375°, Reg. 5–6) for 35 to 40 mins.

Serve immediately. Any soufflé will collapse after it has risen
to its maximum height.

Mushroom Soufflé. For 4

Follow the previous recipe, but instead of the grated cheese
add the following:

    1 onion   1 oz. fat
    6 oz. mushrooms

Chop the onion and cut the mushrooms into thin slices. Fry
both together in 1 oz. fat until soft. Strain off any liquid before
adding it to the soufflé mixture.

Cauliflower Soufflé. For 4

Follow the recipe for Cheese Soufflé but, instead of the grated
cheese, add the following:

    1 small cauliflower
    ½ oz. fat

After washing divide the cauliflower into its small flowerets.
Melt the fat in a saucepan, add the cauliflower and stew over a
low heat for about 5 mins., shaking the saucepan occasionally to
prevent burning. If the cauliflower is still very hard add a little
water, but not more than ½ cup. Strain off any liquid before
adding the cauliflower to the soufflé mixture.

Soufflé Espagnole. For 4

Follow the recipe for Cheese Soufflé but, instead of the grated
cheese, add the following:

    1 small green pepper   1 tomato
    1 medium onion   ½ oz. fat

Chop the onion, cut the pepper into fine strips and the tomato
into thick slices. Fry all three ingredients together in the fat
until soft. Add no water; on the contrary, drain off any liquid
before adding this to the soufflé mixture.

Spinach Soufflé. For 4

Follow the recipe for Cheese Soufflé but, instead of the grated cheese, add ½ lb. chopped raw spinach. Also reduce the quantity of milk for the soufflé mixture, using only ¾ pt. Baking time 45 to 50 mins.

Tomato Soufflé. For 4

2 oz. butter or margarine	1 lb. tomatoes
2 oz. flour	4 eggs
¾ pt milk	1 oz. grated cheese

Cut the tomatoes into thick slices. Melt ½ oz. fat in a saucepan, and stew the tomatoes for 5 mins. Strain and keep. Melt the rest of the fat in a saucepan, add the flour, and stew for 2 mins. Add the heated milk (together with a little salt and yeast extract to taste) and cook for another 5 mins., then add the tomatoes and let the mixture cool down. Then follow the recipe for Cheese Soufflé, using only 1 oz. grated cheese.

SAVOURY PASTRIES

Each of these savoury pastry dishes is based on one of the following five pastry recipes. The quantities given are based on flour of 100 per cent (wholemeal) and 81 per cent extraction unless stated otherwise. But flour always varies and, particularly wholemeal, sometimes requires less liquid than given in the recipes.

In some of the following recipes the expression 'baking blind' is used. This means that the pastry should be partly baked before the filling is added. There are two possible methods of preventing the pastry from rising during this 'blind' baking. Either prick a number of holes in it with a fork, or cover it with a sheet of greaseproof paper held down by a layer of white beans.

Short Pastry

6 oz. flour	3 oz. butter or margarine
salt optional	3 Tbs. water

Sift the flour into a mixing bowl, cut the fat into small pieces and rub them into the flour with your fingertips until they resemble coarse breadcrumbs. Add the water and knead the mixture lightly into a dough. (Too much handling will make the pastry rather hard.) Let it stand for ½ to 1 hour before using it.

Puff Pastry (1)

8 oz. flour   ½ cup cold water (or less)
6–7 oz. butter   salt optional

All ingredients should be cool. Sift the flour (and a little salt if
desired) into a mixing bowl. Cut the butter into small pieces and
rub them into the flour with your fingertips. Add the cold water
and mix to a stiff dough. Sprinkle some flour on a pastryboard
and roll the dough into an oblong sheet about ½ inch thick. Brush
off all loose flour. Then fold one third over on top, another
third underneath. Roll the pastry out again, preferably across
(or with the pastry turned round 90 degrees), fold it over as
before and let it rest in a cold place (in the refrigerator if possible)
for 20 to 30 mins. Repeat the rolling out, folding over, and rest-
ing three times. Lastly roll the pastry out and cut it into the
required shapes. It is advisable to let the pastry rest another 20
mins. before being used.

Puff Pastry (2)

8 oz. flour   ½ cup water or a little more
7 oz. butter or margarine   a little salt (optional)

Sift the flour (and salt) into a mixing bowl, add half the butter
in small pieces and rub them into the flour with the fingertips.
Add the water and knead to a smooth, stiff paste. Roll into an
oblong sheet about ½ inch thick and dab the rest of the butter in
small pieces on top of one half of the sheet. Then fold the un-
buttered half over, turn the pastry round, and roll it out again.
Fold it in three, wrap it in a damp cloth, and let it rest in a cold
place for 1½ to 2 hours. Then roll it out again, fold it in three, and
let it rest again for 2 hours in a cold place. This has to be repeated
once more, and then the pastry will be ready for use.

Yeast Pastry

5–6 oz. flour   ⅛ oz. yeast*
1 oz. fat   4 Tbs. warm milk

Put the flour (and salt if desired) in a large mixing bowl in a

---

* If dry yeast is used, follow the manufacturer's instruction.

warm place. (The flour can of course be warmed in its paper bag and then put into the bowl.) Add the fat, in small pieces. Make a well in the middle and pour in 2 Tbs. of the warm milk in which the yeast has been dissolved. Stir with a wooden spoon, starting from the centre until the milk and some of the flour forms a fairly thick paste. Then cover the bowl with a towel and leave it in a warm place until the paste in the centre of the bowl has risen to double its original size (30 to 45 mins.). Then add the rest of the milk and knead hard (about 10 mins.) until you are sure that the ingredients, particularly the yeast, are evenly distributed. Then leave it in a warm place again and let the dough rise to double its size; it can then be rolled out and used for baking.

Choux Pastry

4 oz. flour	3 small eggs
2 oz. butter or margarine	¼ pt boiling water

For choux pastry a good plain white flour gives best results but 81 per cent wholemeal can also be used.

Put the butter in a saucepan and add the boiling water. Stir in the dry flour and beat hard until the mixture is smooth, fairly thick, and leaves the sides of the saucepan. Take the pan off the flame and let it cool a little (so that the eggs which come next do not set). Beat one egg in at a time and do not add the next egg before the previous one is properly mixed in. This is a very useful paste; it can be used for both sweet and savoury dishes, and can be 'piped' on a baking tin or dropped a spoonful at a time into deep fat and fried, and used, for example, for garnishes or cocktail savouries.

Cheese Tart with Curd Cheese. For 4

Short Pastry (page 143)	½ cup milk
8 oz. curd cheese	1 Tbs. cream (optional)
1½ Tbs. flour	chopped chives or
2 small eggs	spring onions

Roll out the pastry to about ⅛ inch thickness, covering the bottom and rim of a 8 to 9 inch round baking tin, and bake 'blind' for

10 mins. in a hot oven (450°, Reg. 9). For the filling rub the curd cheese through a sieve, add the flour and milk (and cream), a little salt If desired, and the yolks of the eggs. Mix well. Whip the egg whites to a stiff froth and fold carefully into the cheese mixture together with the chives. Fill the pastry case and bake in a moderate oven (350°, Reg. 4–5) for 40 to 50 mins.

Cheese Tart with Cheddar Cheese. For 4

Short Pastry (page 143)
4 oz. grated cheese
1 oz. flour
salt and nutmeg to taste

2 small or 1 large egg
1½ cups milk (or half milk, half cream)

As previous recipe, but the filling is made as follows. Whisk all ingredients together and pile into the case. If desired, the egg can be separated and the whipped froth of the egg whites folded into the mixture.

Mushroom Tart. For 4

The same as Cheese Tart but with the filling as follows:

6 oz. mushrooms
1 medium onion
1 oz. fat

2 eggs
1 cup milk
1 oz. flour

Cut the cleaned mushrooms into thin slices. Chop the onion. Melt the fat in a frying pan and fry the onions and mushrooms for about 5 mins. Whisk the milk, flour, and eggs together, add seasoning if desired. Spread the mushrooms and onions over the bottom of the tart case and pour the egg mixture over it. Bake in a moderate oven (350°, Reg. 4 or 5) for 40 to 45 mins.

Onion Tart. For 4

Short Pastry (page 143) made from ½ lb. flour, 4 oz. butter or margarine, and 4 Tbs. water.

Filling
1 lb. onions
1 oz. flour
1 oz. fat

1 cup milk
½ cup cream or top of milk
2 small eggs
salt to taste

Make a tart case by lining a baking tin as in Cheese Tart recipe (page 145) but with bottom and sides thicker ($\frac{1}{4}$ inch). Bake 'blind' for 15 mins. in a hot oven (400°, Reg. 6). Peel and slice the onions and fry slowly in 1 oz. fat until soft and not yet yellow. Sprinkle the flour over this; whisk the milk, cream, and eggs together and mix with the onions. Fill the pastry case. If any pastry is left over, roll it out, cut it into narrow strips and make a trellis-work pattern on top of the tart. Brush with a little egg or water and bake in a moderate oven (350°, Reg. 5) for about 30 to 35 mins.

Spinach Tart. For 4

Short Pastry from quantities used for Onion Tart (page 146):

Filling

1 lb. spinach	Cream Sauce (page 95)
1 egg	$\frac{1}{2}$ cup milk
2 Tbs. cream	nutmeg and salt to taste

Make a tart case and bake 'blind' as in the previous recipe. Make creamed spinach as on page 68, spread on the pastry. Whisk egg, milk, and cream together and pour over the spinach. Bake in moderate oven (350°, Reg. 5) for 25 to 30 mins.

Mixed Vegetable Tart. For 4   DELISH

Short Pastry from quantities used for Onion Tart (page 146):

Filling

$\frac{1}{2}$ stick celery	1 large onion
2 carrots*	1 oz. fat
4 oz. cauliflower*	1 cup Béchamel Sauce (p. 96)
4 oz. peas*	1 tsp. yeast extract
4 oz. beans*	1 oz. grated cheese —MORE.

Wash and peel the vegetables in the usual way. The carrots are sliced, the celery cut into small pieces, the cauliflower divided into flowerets, the onion chopped. Fry the onions and carrots slightly in the fat, and boil the other vegetables, preferably separately, until they are nearly – but not quite – soft. Mix and spread over the pastry. Pour a cup of thin béchamel sauce over

* Or any other vegetables except potatoes.

4 OZ CAULI
3 LEEKS   LARGE TIN
1 16 SPROUTS
PEAS

the vegetables and top with grated cheese. Bake in a moderate oven (400°, Reg. 6) for 20 to 30 mins.

Vegetable Pie. For 4

Short Pastry from quantities used for Onion Tart (page 146):

Mixed vegetables (as in the   2 large potatoes
   previous recipe)   1 tsp. yeast extract
1 cup stock or water

Prepare and cook the vegetables as in the previous recipe and place them in a pie dish. Heat the stock (or water), mix it with the yeast extract and seasoning if desired, pour this over the vegetables, and finally cover them with a layer of sliced raw potatoes. An egg cup or a pie funnel should be placed in the centre of the dish. (This helps to let the steam escape, while the raw potatoes act as a buffer to prevent the pastry on top from getting soggy.) Roll out the pastry, fairly thin, about $\frac{1}{8}$ inch. Cut off a strip as wide as the edge of the pie dish and cover the edge with it. Then cover the whole pie dish with the pastry and press it down – with a fork to make a decorative pattern – round the edge. Brush the top with water or an egg yolk, cut a small hole or cross in the centre (for the steam to escape) and bake in a hot oven (400–425°, Reg. 6–7) for 45 mins.

Mushroom Pie. For 4

Short Pastry from quantities used for Onion Tart (page 146):

Filling
1$\frac{1}{2}$ lb. mushrooms   2 large cooked potatoes
2 or 3 onions   1 tsp. yeast extract
$\frac{1}{2}$ pt stock or water (or milk)   1 bayleaf
1$\frac{1}{4}$ oz. flour   salt to taste
2$\frac{1}{2}$ oz. fat

Wash and slice the mushrooms. Peel and chop the onions. Melt 1 oz. fat in a saucepan and stew the mushrooms, onions, and bayleaf together (without water). When the mushrooms begin to soften (after 3 to 5 mins.) take the pan off flame and strain. Keep the mushroom water. Melt the rest of the fat in a saucepan separately, add the flour, and stew for 2 to 3 mins., stirring all the time. Add the stock, milk or water, and mushroom water, salt if desired, and yeast extract and cook for another 7 to 10 mins. Then add the mushrooms, the diced potatoes and onions, mix and put into pie dish. Cover with pastry and bake as in previous recipe for 30 mins.

Cheese Patties. For 4

Short Pastry (page 143)
Filling

3 oz. grated cheese	2 eggs
½ oz. flour	nutmeg and salt to taste
1 cup milk or half milk, half cream	chopped parsley

Roll out the pastry fairly thin and cut into rounds, big enough to fill patty tins. Bake them 'blind' in these tins for 5 to 10 mins. in a hot oven. For the filling just whisk all the ingredients together, adding the cheese and parsley last. Fill the patty tins half full (the mixture will rise) and bake in a moderate oven (350°, Reg. 4–5) for 30 mins. or until the patty tops are well browned.

Mushroom and Tomato Turnovers. For 4

Short Pastry (page 143)
Filling

⅓ lb. mushrooms	1 tsp. chopped herbs such as
1 large onion	parsley, chives, sage, marjoram
2 large tomatoes	joram
1 egg	salt to taste
1 oz. fat	

Melt the fat in a shallow saucepan, add the chopped onion, and stew it for 2 to 3 mins. Add the sliced mushrooms and stew for another 5 mins. Lastly add the cubed tomatoes and herbs and stew for another 2 mins. Strain off any liquid.

Roll out the pastry fairly thin and cut out round pieces using a saucer. Place a ½ Tbs. of the mushroom-tomato mixture in the centre of each round, paint the edges with whisked egg, fold over and press the edges firmly together. Paint the top half with egg and bake in a hot oven (425–450°, Reg. 7–8) for about 20 to 25 mins. or until the tops are well browned.

Cornish Pasties. For 4

Short Pastry (page 143)
Filling

2 hard-boiled eggs	2 oz. fat
½ lb. potatoes	1 raw egg
1 tomato	2 or 3 sliced mushrooms
1 small onion	(optional)
1 gherkin	

Melt ½ oz. fat and fry the chopped onion and mushrooms together for 3 to 5 mins. Strain off any liquid. Heat the remaining fat (1½ oz.), add the raw potatoes in thin slices, and fry them covered with a lid until they are fairly soft, turning them over occasionally. Chop the tomato and gherkin. Roll out the pastry fairly thin and cut out round pieces with a saucer. Place into each round: a few slices of the boiled egg, a few potato slices, a little mushroom and a little of the gherkin and tomato. Paint the edge of the pastry round with the whisked raw egg, fold over, and press the edges together. The traditional method is to lift opposite sides of the pastry rounds and press the edges firmly between the thumb and forefinger, making two cuts with a sharp knife on top. Brush with egg and bake in a hot oven (450°, Reg. 7 or 8) for 25 to 30 mins. or until the tops are well browned.

Baked Savoury Roll. For 4

Short Pastry from ½ lb. flour, 4 oz. butter, and 4 Tbs. water.

Filling

¼ small cabbage*	1 tsp. mixed herbs
1 onion*	1 oz. fat
2 carrots*	1 tsp. yeast extract
1 leek*	1 tsp. flour or cornflour
1 tomato*	1 oz. grated nuts
a few mushrooms*	½ egg

Chop or mince all the vegetables finely. Melt the fat in a saucepan and stew the minced vegetables in it for about 10 mins., stirring from time to time. Then take off the flame and add the nuts, herbs, yeast extract, and flour. Mix well and cool.

* Or similar combination of vegetables.

Roll the pastry out into a large square, about ⅛ inch thick, and spread the minced vegetable mixture evenly over it. Leave the edges free and paint them with the whisked raw egg. Then roll up the pastry with the vegetables, fold the sides over and press them down. Paint the top and sides with egg and, if desired, sprinkle a little salt on top. Bake in a hot oven (400–425°, Reg. 6 or 7) for 30 to 40 mins. or until the top is brown. Serve with gravy (page 96).

Mushroom Egg Roll

As in the previous recipe but with a different filling, namely:

4 hard-boiled eggs	1 oz. fat
½ lb. mushrooms	1 raw egg
2 medium onions	salt to taste

Peel the boiled eggs and chop them finely. Cut the mushrooms and onions into thin slices and fry them in the fat for 8 to 10 mins. Strain off any liquid and let it cool. Then proceed as in the preceding recipe but spread the egg first on the pastry and then the mushrooms and onion as a second layer. (The dry hard-boiled egg will act as a buffer and prevent the pastry from getting soggy.) The raw egg is used for painting the roll.

Filled Vol-au-Vents

These are pastry cases made of puff pastry, which are then filled with, for example, Creamed Mushrooms (page 63), Buttered Peas (page 66), Mixed Vegetable Dish (page 89), or anything else which seems suitable. They can be bought ready for filling from the baker, but here is a recipe for home-made vol-au-vent cases.

Puff Pastry (page 143) plus 1 egg

Roll out the pastry, about ¼ inch thick. Cut out with a round 3 inch pastry cutter twice as many pieces as the number of pastry cases required. Place half of these (the case bottoms) on a baking sheet. Out of the remaining rounds cut lids, using a smaller round cutter, and place them on a baking sheet to be baked separately. The remaining rings (the sides of the pastry case) are then carefully stuck flat on the case bottoms, using plain water or an egg white as glue. With the raw egg yolk, paint the lids and the tops of the rings, the latter very carefully so that no egg yolk runs down the sides inside or outside, as this would prevent the puff pastry from rising properly. Bake in a hot oven (425°, Reg. 8) for 15 to 20 mins.

Pizza Napolitana. For 4

Yeast Pastry (page 144)	a little oil
5–6 ripe tomatoes	1 tsp. chopped thyme or
3 oz. Cheddar cheese	oregano

Roll out the yeast pastry about ¼ inch thick. Place either the whole rolled out sheet or individual rounds, cut about 5 to 6 inches in diameter, on a baking sheet. Leave them in a warm place and let them rise to about double height. Then brush a little oil over the surface and cover it with skinned tomato slices. (To remove the skins, put the tomatoes for a minute in boiling water, and they will then come off easily.) Then the sliced cheese is distributed over the surface, which is again painted with a little oil and finally topped with a sprinkling of the herbs. Bake in a fairly hot oven (400°, Reg. 6 or 7) for 15 to 20 mins. Serve hot.

Savoury Éclairs. For 4

Choux Pastry (page 145)
Filling

⅛ lb. mushrooms	2 oz. fat
2 Tbs. cooked peas	1½ oz. flour
1 onion	1 cup stock or water

Put the choux pastry in a piping bag with a large (½ inch) nozzle and pipe it in straight lengths about 3 inches long on a floured baking sheet, allowing some space between the strips. Bake them in a moderate oven (350–375°, Reg. 5 or 6) for 15 mins. or until light brown. Keep them hot. Make the filling as follows. Slice the mushrooms, chop the onion, and fry both together in 1 oz. fat for 10 mins. Melt the remaining fat in a saucepan, add the flour, stew for a few minutes, add the stock or water and stew for another 5 to 7 mins., stirring all the time. This sauce should be thick but if it is too stiff a little water or mushroom water can be added. Then add the mushrooms, onions, cooked peas, and seasoning, if required, to the sauce and mix. Cut the éclairs in half and sandwich the filling between. Serve hot.

Cheese Puffs. For 4

Choux Pastry (page 145)   1 oz. Parmesan or other cheese
                                               oil for frying

Make a choux pastry, but mix 1 oz. grated cheese to the mixture. Heat some oil in a strong large frying pan (or in a deep-fry pan) but do not let it get too hot. Test the heat by dropping a Tbs. of the mixture into the oil and fry slowly until evenly brown. This is a sign that the oil is just hot enough to continue with the rest of the mixture, dropping it into the oil spoon by spoon.

Vegetable Sausage Rolls. For 6 to 8

Short Pastry from ½ lb. flour,   1 egg
  4 oz. butter, and 4 Tbs.   2 Tbs. milk
  water   a little oil
Nut Rissole mixture (page 135)
  (without dipping it and
  without breadcrumbs)

Shape little sausages about 2 inches long from the rissole mixture, roll them in flour, and fry them in oil on both sides until they are light brown. Let them cool. Roll out the short pastry ¼ inch thick, cut into rectangles 3 by 4 inches. Place a 'sausage' in each and roll the pastry round them. Whisk the egg and milk together and paint the edges of the pastry with it. Then fold the sides over, press them together, and paint the top and sides. Bake in a hot oven (400°, Reg. 7) for 15 to 20 mins. or until the pastry is brown.

OTHER MAIN COURSE DISHES

Fried Cabbage Slices. For 4

1 medium firm cabbage   garlic or garlic salt
¼ cup oil   ¼ pt stock or water

Cut the cabbage in half and wash carefully. Drain and dry it
with a towel. Cut into ½ inch slices. Heat the oil in a frying pan,
add a clove of chopped garlic, and fry the cabbage slices for a
few minutes on both sides. Pour the stock or water into a fireproof dish and put the fried cabbage slices in it side by side, add
a little salt and bake in a hot oven (400°, Reg. 6) for 15 mins.
Then put a sheet of greaseproof paper over the dish (to prevent
it from drying out) and continue baking for another 20 to 30
mins. until the cabbage is soft.

Cauliflower Pudding (baked). For 4

1 large cauliflower	3 oz. butter or margarine
2 oz. mushrooms	2 eggs
4 oz. oat flakes	1 oz. grated cheese
1 onion	salt to taste

Wash the cauliflower (see page 54) and divide it into its flowerets.
Boil until nearly soft and strain. Chop the onions and mushrooms.
Melt 2 oz. of the butter in a deep frying pan and stew the mushrooms, onions, and oats in it without water for about 10 to 15
mins. Let the mixture cool. Cream the remaining butter and add
two egg yolks. Mix everything together, and lastly fold in the
stiffly whisked egg whites. Put the mixture in a greased fireproof
dish, top with grated cheese, and bake in a moderately hot oven
(400°, Reg. 5) for 35 to 40 mins.

Spinach Pudding (steamed). For 4

1 lb. spinach	½ pt hot milk
6 oz. stale bread or rolls	3 Tbs. breadcrumbs
4 eggs	nutmeg and salt to taste
2 oz. butter	

Wash the spinach carefully, chop it finely and stew it in the butter
for 7 to 10 mins. until fairly soft. Cut the bread or rolls into small
pieces and soak them in the hot milk. By the time it is cool the
milk will probably have been absorbed; but if it has not, squeeze
out the surplus moisture. Also squeeze out any surplus liquid
from the spinach. Mix the bread and spinach with the 4 egg
yolks and add the seasoning. Whisk the egg whites to a stiff froth

and fold them into the spinach mixture. Grease a pudding basin and cover the sides and bottom with some of the breadcrumbs. Add the pudding mixture but do not fill the basin more than two-thirds full. Sprinkle the remaining breadcrumbs on top, cover with a pudding cloth or greaseproof paper and steam for at least an hour. Turn the pudding out on to a hot plate. Serve with Tomato Sauce (page 101).

Mushroom Pudding. For 4

6 oz. mushrooms	2 oz. butter
1 medium onion	2 eggs
6 oz. stale bread	chopped parsley
3 Tbs. breadcrumbs	salt to taste

Cut the bread into large cubes and wet it thoroughly in hot water. Squeeze out all surplus moisture. Fry the thinly sliced mushrooms in a little butter for 5 mins. Chop the onion. Melt the rest of the butter in a deep frying pan, add the bread, onion, and parsley, and fry, stirring with a wooden spoon until the mixture comes off the sides of the frying pan easily. Empty into a mixing bowl, add the mushrooms, salt, and egg yolks, and mix well. Whisk the egg whites to a stiff froth and fold it carefully into the mixture. Then proceed exactly as in previous recipe.

Leek Pie. For 4

1 lb. leeks	Cream Sauce (page 95)
1 lb. potatoes	1 oz. butter

Boil leeks (page 60), mix in cream sauce, and put them in a greased fireproof dish. Cut ¼ lb. of the peeled potatoes into thin slices, fry them in ½ oz. butter until nearly – but not quite – soft, and put them on top of the leeks. Then use the remaining potatoes to make a stiff purée of mashed potatoes (that is, using less liquid than usual) and spread it on top of the sliced potatoes. Cut the remaining ½ oz. butter into small pieces on top and bake in moderate oven (375°, Reg. 5) for 25 to 30 mins.

Shepherd's Pie. For 4

[handwritten note: DON'T MAKE TOO SLOPPY]
[handwritten note: LOVELY]
[handwritten checkmark]

2 medium carrots*	2 oz. butter or fat
2 small turnips*	½ pt stock or water
2 leeks*	2 oz. nuts (hazels)
2 onions	1 oz. flour
1 lb. potatoes	1 tsp. yeast extract

Wash, prepare, and cook the vegetables, except the onions, in a little water until quite soft. Cook the potatoes separately, and mash them into a stiff purée. Mash the other cooked vegetables separately or put them through a mincer. Fry the chopped onion in ¼ oz. fat. Roast the nuts as described on page 135, and grate them. Then melt 1 oz. fat in a saucepan, add the flour, stew for 2 mins., add the stock (or water) and cook for another 5 mins. Then mix the yeast extract, grated nuts, and half the fried onions into this mixture, and the other half of the onions into the mashed vegetables. Grease a fireproof dish and place first the mashed vegetables in it, then the nut mixture and finally the mashed potatoes. Make a pattern by criss-crossing with a fork. (Alternatively the potatoes can be 'piped' on.) Top with small pieces of the remaining butter and bake ½ hour in a moderate oven (350°, Reg. 5).

Tomato Oat Cakes. For 4

4 oz. rolled oats	4 Tbs. water
1 Tbs. tomato purée	1 tsp. chopped chives
2 tomatoes	oil for frying
1 onion	1 egg or 1 tsp. soya flour (optional)

Soak the oats in 4 Tbs. water, mix in the tomato purée and let the mixture stand for 15 mins. In the meantime chop the onion and cut the tomatoes into small cubes. Then add these to the oat mixture together with the egg (or 1 tsp. soya flour), chives, and salt if desired, and mix well. The mixture should be fairly soft. Heat the oil in a frying pan, drop 1 Tbs. of the mixture into it, and spread it out slightly with the back of a fork. Add as many Tbs. as the frying pan will hold without the cakes sticking

* Or any similar combination of vegetables.

together. Fry on a low heat so that all the ingredients will cook properly.

Excellent with Creamed Spinach (page 68).

Lentil Kromeskies. For 4 or 5

2 oz. cooked lentils	1½ oz. fat
(from 1 oz. dry)	4 oz. mushrooms
1 oz. flour	¼ pt stock or water
1 oz. breadcrumbs	½ cup Batter (page 132)
oil for frying	salt to taste

Chop the mushrooms and add them to the cooked lentils. Melt the fat in a saucepan, add the flour and stew for 2 mins., then add the stock or water, stirring all the time. Cook until it becomes a very thick sauce which easily peels off the sides of the saucepan. Take the pan off the flame, add the lentils, breadcrumbs, and salt, mix well, and cool. Then shape or cut the mixture into 8 or 10 pieces, dip them in the batter mixture and fry in deep fat until golden brown.

Stuffed Vine Leaves. For 4 or 5

8 or 10 large fresh vine leaves	fat for frying
3 oz. rice	

Wash the leaves and dip them for 1 min. in boiling water. Boil the rice in plain water (with perhaps a little salt added) until soft but not mashy. Run cold water over it. Put 1 Tbs. of rice in the centre of each leaf, then roll them up, tuck the sides neatly underneath and fry them slowly in a frying pan. They can also be baked side by side in a well-oiled fireproof dish (350°, Reg. 5) for 30 mins.

Note that no seasoning should be used; the vine leaves transmit a very delicate flavour to the rice which any seasoning would spoil.

Bavarian Dumplings. For 4

3 brown rolls or equivalent	1½ oz. fat
bread	nutmeg and salt to taste
2 Tbs. flour or breadcrumbs	½ cup milk
½ tsp. chopped parsley	1 small onion
2 eggs	

Cut half the bread or rolls into medium cubes and fry them in the fat together with the chopped onion until the bread is light brown. Cut the rest of the bread into pieces and soak them in hot milk. Add salt and nutmeg and mash the bread. Then put everything into a mixing bowl and mix to a thick dough. Form balls, each from 1 heaped Tbs. of the dough, and cook them in boiling salted water for about 20 mins. Place only enough dumplings into the water to allow each to swell while cooking.

Can be served cut in half with melted butter or whole with Horseradish Sauce (page 99).

Swiss Vegetable Dumplings. For 4 to 6

1 medium carrot	3 thick slices bread
2 large mushrooms	½ cup milk
1 small onion	1 Tbs. breadcrumbs
1 Tbs. cooked green peas	1 Tbs. flour
2 eggs	1 oz. butter
1 tsp. chopped parsley	salt and nutmeg to taste

Cut the carrot, onion, and mushrooms into small cubes and cook the onion and carrot together, the mushrooms separately, in very little water until nearly soft. Strain them. Cut the bread in small pieces and soak them in the hot milk. When soft, mash it or put it through a mincer, and add cooked vegetables, eggs, salt, and nutmeg. Pour the melted butter over the mixture and finally add the breadcrumbs and flour and mix it all to a thick dough. Then form balls and proceed as in previous recipe, except that the dumplings can be a little smaller.

Boulettes à la Chartreuse (Charterhouse Dumplings). For 4

3 thick slices bread	½ cup hot milk
1 brown roll	1 Tbs. milk
1 onion	2 Tbs. breadcrumbs
4 oz. mushrooms	2 eggs
1 oz. fat	salt or garlic salt

Cut the bread into pieces and soak them in the hot milk. When it is soft mash it or put it through a mincer. Fry the chopped onion and mushrooms together in the fat until soft and add them to the soaked bread. Add the roll, cut into small cubes, to the mixture, also 1 egg, and the salt or garlic salt. Mix this to a stiff dough; if it is not stiff enough add some flour. Divide it into four portions and form each into a big ball. Boil them in salt water for 30 to 35 mins. Then take them out of the water and let them cool. Paint them with the other egg whisked together with the milk, cover them with breadcrumbs, and fry them in deep fat.

Semolina Dumplings. For 4

4 oz. coarse semolina	1 egg
1½ pt water, or milk and	1 oz. fat
water mixed	2–3 Tbs. breadcrumbs
1 oz. grated cheese	salt to taste

Bring the water (or milk and water) to the boil and pour in the semolina, stirring all the time. (If salt is desired, add this first.) Cook for 15 to 20 mins., then let it cool down a little, add the egg and cheese, and mix. Form dumplings either by hand or with a spoon and drop these into boiling water. Simmer until the dumplings rise to the surface. Take them out with a perforated spoon or ladle and place on a hot dish. In the meantime fry the breadcrumbs in the fat and sprinkle these over the dumplings before serving.

Onion Rings

Mainly decorative and very tasty and light.

4 oz. flour	1 egg
2 oz. fat	2 Tbs. milk
1 large onion	breadcrumbs
2 Tbs. water	oil for frying

Chop the onion finely. Rub the fat into the flour with the finger-tips until the mixture resembles fine breadcrumbs. Add the water and mix into a stiff dough with the onions. Roll the dough out to about ¼ inch thick and cut out rings with 2½ inch and 1½ inch round cutters. Dip the rings into the egg and milk whisked together, cover with breadcrumbs, and fry in deep fat – not too hot – until golden brown.

The inner cut-out rounds make tasty savoury biscuits. Paint

them with egg, put them on a greased baking sheet, and bake
(350°, Reg. 5) for 15 mins.

QUICK SAVOURIES

As mentioned on page 16 ready-cooked foods in packets and
tins are obtainable from health food stores. Keep a few in the
larder and they will come in handy when you are pressed for
time or a visitor stays for a meal unexpectedly. Then there are
the usual stand-by dishes of fried, poached, or scrambled eggs
and omelettes (page 137) which are made quickly. But some
more interesting dishes with or without eggs are given in this
section.

Poached Egg (made without an egg-poacher)

Add 1 tsp. vinegar and a little salt to 2 inches of water in a saucepan. Bring to the boil. Break the egg carefully into a cup and
slide it slowly into the water. More than one egg can be poached
in the saucepan at a time. When they are set (after 2 to 3 mins.
vigorous boiling) take them out with a perforated spoon or ladle.

Poached Egg and Cheshire Cheese on Toast. For 1

For reasons of their own the French call this *œuf à l'anglaise*.

1 round toast	1 tsp. butter
1 or 2 eggs	½ Tbs. grated Cheshire cheese

Spread half the butter on the hot toast, and put the poached
egg(s) carefully on it. Top with the grated cheese and the
remainder of the butter (melted). Grill until the top is well
browned.

Poached Egg Comtesse. For 1

1 round toast	2 asparagus tips
1 or 2 eggs	a little butter
2 medium mushrooms	a little salt

Butter the toast and poach the egg(s). Cut the mushrooms in
half and grill them. Put the egg(s) on the toast, top with the
grilled mushrooms, and garnish with asparagus tips.

Scrambled Eggs. For 1

2 eggs	1 tsp. (level) flour
½ oz. fat	1½ Tbs. milk

Whisk together the eggs, flour, and milk, and add salt if desired. Heat the fat in a frying pan, pour in the egg mixture, reduce the heat, and stir with a fork constantly but not too vigorously, until the mixture is almost set. (It will set completely after being taken off the flame.)

Scrambled Egg with Tomatoes. For 1

2 eggs	1 oz. fat
1 large tomato	1 tsp. (level) flour
½ onion	1½ Tbs. milk

Heat ½ oz. fat in a frying pan, add the chopped onion and tomato and fry for about 5 mins. Add the remaining fat. Make the scrambled egg mixture (egg, milk, and flour), pour it into the frying pan, and stir until the eggs are set.

Scrambled Egg with Mushrooms. For 1

2 eggs	1 oz. fat
3 medium mushrooms	1 tsp. (level) flour
½ onion	1½ Tbs. milk

Heat ½ oz. fat in a frying pan, add the chopped onion and fry for 2 mins., then add the mushrooms cut into thick slices and fry for another 3 mins. Then proceed as in the previous recipe.

Spanish Egg on Toast. For 1

½ green pepper	1 egg
1 medium onion	1 oz. fat
1 round buttered toast	salt to taste

Chop the pepper and onion and fry them in ½ oz. fat until soft (6 to 8 mins.). Take the mixture carefully out of the frying pan and put it on the toast. Keep it hot. Fry the egg in the remaining fat (reduce the heat), place it on top of the toast, and serve.

Eggburger. For 1

1 soft roll	1 oz. fat
1 egg	1 thin slice Cheddar cheese

Cut the roll in half and lightly toast the cut side of both halves. In the meantime melt the fat in a frying pan and fry the egg lightly on both sides. Pour a little of the fat on one half of the roll and put the cheese on the other, and toast this one under the grill for another minute or two. Then put the fried egg on the other half-roll and cover with the cheese half. Serve hot.

Devilled Egg on Toast. For 1

1 whole egg	1 round buttered or
1 egg yolk	dry toast
1 oz. butter	1 tsp. made-up mustard
2 Tbs. milk	2 heaped tsp. chutney

Poach the whole egg. In the meantime melt the butter in a saucepan and add the milk, mustard, and chutney (and any other seasoning desired), stirring all the time over a low heat. When hot stir in the beaten egg yolk until the mixture has thickened (which will take only a minute or two). This is now the devilled sauce. Place the poached egg on the toast and cover with the sauce. Serve hot.

Mushrooms, Tomatoes, and Fried Egg on Toast. For 1

1 round buttered toast	1 large tomato
1 egg	1 oz. fat
2 large mushrooms	½ Tbs. flour
½ small onion	salt to taste

Cut the mushrooms into thin slices and chop the onion. Melt ½ oz. fat in a frying pan, add the onion and fry for 1 to 2 mins., then add the mushrooms and fry for another 5 mins. Sprinkle the flour over this and cook for another 2 mins. when the mixture will thicken. Grill the tomato halves without fat. Keep the mushrooms and tomato hot. Use the remaining fat for frying the egg (one side only). Place the mushrooms on the toast, then the tomato halves and top with the fried egg.

Mushrooms and Tomatoes on Toast. For 1

Exactly as in the previous recipe but without the egg (and using only ½ oz. fat).

Egg à la Monte Carlo. For 4

4 slices of fried bread	Tomato Sauce (page 102)
2 oz. fat or oil	4 eggs

Keep the fried bread hot. Fry the eggs in 2 oz. fat, butter, or oil, on both sides. Place a fried egg in the middle of each slice of fried bread and cover the whole with plenty of hot and thick tomato sauce (which when served in Monte Carlo is very thick and contains a good helping of garlic).

Baked Eggs à la Mornay. For 2

4 whole eggs	1 oz. fat
1 egg yolk	1½ oz. flour
1 oz. grated cheese	½ pt stock or milk

To make a sauce, melt the fat in a saucepan, then add the flour and stew for 2 mins., stirring all the time. Add the stock or milk and cook for another 5 mins. (still stirring), then take the pan off the flame and let it cool a little. Beat the egg yolk and fold carefully into the sauce. Grease a fireproof dish, or two individual ones each big enough to hold two eggs comfortably. Pour half the sauce into it or them. Break each egg carefully into a cup and slip it slowly on to the sauce in the dish(es). Then pour the remaining sauce into the dish(es) trying not to cover the egg yolks. Sprinkle the grated cheese over the dishes (with a thicker layer over the eggs) and bake them in a moderate oven (350–375°, Reg. 4) for 15 mins. (for soft eggs) or 20 mins. (for hard ones).

Creamed Eggs. For 2

3 hard-boiled eggs	2 Tbs. flour
1 oz. butter or fat	2 rounds fried bread (optional)
1 pt milk and water	chopped parsley
or milk only	salt to taste

Shell the eggs and keep them hot. Melt the butter or fat in a saucepan, add the flour and stew for 2 mins., stirring all the time. Add the milk (and water) and the salt if desired, and cook for another 5 to 7 mins., still stirring. Place the eggs on a hot dish and pour the sauce over them. If desired, cut the fried bread into 1 inch strips and place round the dish. Before serving sprinkle with chopped parsley.

Eggs Florentine. For 2

This is a useful dish when there is some spinach left over (preferably leaf spinach, page 67).

cooked spinach (from 1 lb. raw spinach)	1 oz. fat
	1 oz. flour
4 eggs	½ pt milk or water
2 oz. grated cheese	salt and nutmeg to taste

Melt the fat in a saucepan, add the flour and stew for 2 mins. Add the milk or water and cook for another 5 to 7 mins., stirring all the time. Take off the flame and mix in half of the cheese. Poach the eggs lightly. Put the hot spinach in a fireproof dish, place the eggs on top and cover everything with the sauce. Then top with grated cheese, and grill until the top is well browned.

Fried Cheese Sandwich. For 2 or 3

4 or 6 slices bread (¼ inch)	1½ Tbs. flour
2 oz. grated cheese	1 cup milk
1 egg	2 Tbs. breadcrumbs
½ Tbs. fat	oil for frying

Melt the fat in a saucepan, add the flour and stew for 1 to 2 mins. Add ½ cup milk and cook for another 5 mins., stirring all the time. Take off the flame and add the grated cheese. This should make a fairly thick mixture. Let it cool (but not get quite cold), spread it on 2 (or 3) slices of bread, and cover each with a dry slice. Take care not to squeeze the mixture out at the sides. Whisk the raw egg and the other ½ cup of milk together, add a little salt, dip the sandwiches in this and cover them with breadcrumbs. Fry them in deep fat or oil until golden brown. Serve whole or cut in strips.

Cheese Beignets. For 4

½ lb. Cheddar cheese
(as dry as possible)

Beignet Batter (page 129)
oil or fat for frying

Cut the cheese into pieces about 2½ by 1½ by ¾ inch. Dip them in the batter and fry them in very hot deep fat (or oil) until golden brown. If the fat is not hot enough the batter mixture will not seal the cheese which may become rubbery.

Welsh Rarebit. For 4

4 slices toast
5 oz. grated cheese
1½ Tbs. butter

1 tsp. made-up mustard
3 Tbs. milk
pinch of paprika pepper

Melt the butter in a small saucepan and add the milk, paprika, mustard, and 4 oz. grated cheese. Stew gently over a low heat, stirring until the mixture is smooth; it should also be rather thick. Spread it on the toast, top with a sprinkling of the remaining 1 oz. grated cheese, and brown under hot grill.

Buck Rarebit

As in the previous recipe but with the addition of one poached egg on top of each Welsh rarebit.

Quick Cheese Soufflé. For 1

1 egg
2 tsp. flour (preferably
    self-raising)
½ cup milk

¾ oz. grated cheese
½ oz. fat
salt to taste

Whisk the egg, milk, and flour together and fry like scrambled egg. When nearly set top with grated cheese and brown under a hot grill.

If this is for more than one person or if you do not like to serve it straight from the frying pan, transfer the scrambled egg into a fireproof dish (or small individual dishes), top with grated cheese, and grill.

Mushrooms on Toast. For 1

1 round of buttered toast	1 small onion
2 large mushrooms	1 Tbs. Cream Sauce (page 95)
½ oz. fat	(optional)

Chop the onion and slice the mushrooms thinly and fry them together in ½ oz. fat for 5 mins. Put them on the buttered toast and serve. If cream sauce is being used, mix it with the mushrooms and onions and heat it up again before spreading it on the buttered toast.

Mushrooms Paulette. For 2

2 slices of dry toast	chopped parsley
4 large mushrooms	2 Tbs. Cheese Sauce (page 97)
1 tomato	1 oz. grated cheese
1 oz. fat	6–8 asparagus tips (optional)

Cut the mushrooms into thin slices and fry in 1 oz. fat for 5 mins. Heat the cheese sauce. Place the mushroom slices on the toast and, if any hot fat is left in the frying pan, pour it over the mushrooms. Keep a few mushroom slices for decoration later. Then pour the hot cheese sauce over the toast, sprinkle with the grated cheese, and decorate with the left-over mushroom slices, leaving enough space for thick slices of tomatoes which should now be placed between them. Grill until the cheese is brown and the tomatoes are cooked. If a specially decorative dish is required, top with warmed asparagus tips and garnish with a little chopped parsley.

Onion Cheese Toast. For 1

1 slice of buttered toast	½ oz. fat
1 onion	1 Tbs. grated cheese

Slice the onion into rings and fry in the fat until brown and crisp. Put them on the hot buttered toast, top with the grated cheese, and grill them until the cheese turns light brown.

Stuffed Tomatoes. For 4

4 tomatoes	½ oz. fat
2 oz. grated cheese	a little salt (optional)
2 oz. breadcrumbs	

Cut the tomatoes in half, scoop out the soft part and chop it finely. Mix it with the grated cheese, breadcrumbs, and salt and fill the tomato halves with this mixture. Melt the fat in a fire-proof dish, place the filled tomatoes in it side by side, and bake them in a moderate oven (350°, Reg. 4) for 10 to 15 mins.

Tomato Egg Farci. See page 121.

Semolina Pudding. See page 124.

Farmer's Breakfast. See page 107.

Tomato Oat Cakes. See page 156.

Pancakes. See pages 129 ff.

Uncooked dishes and salads

For those who want to make a radical change in their diet this is the most important section of the book. More and more people are accepting the idea that in order to keep really well – which is more than just avoiding illness – they should eat a good proportion (about fifty per cent) of their food in its natural state, i.e. uncooked and unprocessed. But not only to keep well. Fresh plant food grown on healthy soil has tremendous health-restoring powers. The man who discovered this, long before the importance of vitamins was known, was Dr O. M. Bircher-Benner (1867–1939) who in 1897 founded a sanatorium in Switzerland, now world-famous, where he treated difficult clinical cases successfully with a diet consisting of uncooked vegetables and fruit.

Now, of course, the advice to eat plenty of fresh fruit and vegetables is often given. Yet people still do not always know how to translate this advice into practical terms. This is understandable. Age-long habits cannot be changed overnight, and many people shudder at the thought of raw cabbage leaves and raw carrots replacing their cherished favourite fare. It is true that a fresh fruit-and-vegetable diet will mean that certain stodgy dishes will have to disappear from, or at least appear less often in, our menus. But the uncooked dishes replacing them can be just as delicious.

The successes at the Bircher-Benner sanatorium and our own experience in serving many thousands of uncooked meals in our restaurants have completely convinced us that the little extra trouble taken to prepare such meals will be amply rewarded. Not only will your family enjoy the new régime but good health, vitality, and better resistance to colds and other illnesses will be the long-term result. Twenty-nine different recipes for salad dressings and ninety recipes for uncooked items are given in this section. And of course the main dish of an uncooked meal will consist of two or three items, so, if they are chosen imaginatively, the variety is almost unlimited.

BASIC RULES FOR THE PREPARATION OF UNCOOKED MEALS

(1) *Absolute cleanliness.* In the absence of sterilization through cooking, frequent washing is necessary for all types of leaf vegetables, and additional soaking in salt water is recommended. (The salt can be washed off again later.) If you are at all doubtful, for instance if you are not quite sure that a cucumber skin is really free from insect eggs, dirt, or chemical sprays, sacrifice some of the goodness and peel or scrape the vegetable in question.

(2) *Balance.* A main dish should always include all three basic parts of a plant, namely roots (cauliflower counts as a root), leaves (including celery, leeks), and fruit (including tomatoes and cucumbers).

(3) A *complete menu* may of course include some cooked items, perhaps a soup to begin with, a portion of jacket potatoes or a hot savoury dish with the main (uncooked) course, and a sweet or biscuits and cheese as a third course.

(4) *Dressings and/or sauces* are integral parts of uncooked dishes and should not be treated casually. It cannot be emphasized enough that the widespread hesitation in adopting a diet of uncooked food stems from the knowledge that, without proper dressing, raw carrots, spinach, or cabbage may be liked by rabbits (and children) but are rather a bore for the more sophisticated taste. As the recipes will show, each type of vegetable or fruit has its appropriate dressing; and it would be wrong, as well as dull, to use one type of sauce or dressing for everything.

SALAD DRESSINGS AND COLD SAUCES

For these reasons we deal first with salad dressings, which includes most cold sauces. As a general rule *all* salads should be dressed before being served. This applies even more strictly to uncooked main dishes.

The first four recipes are the basic dressings. Quantities are for suitable amounts and not necessarily only for one salad. It would be rather wasteful to make mayonnaise in such small quantities. Where necessary the quantities needed for individual dressings are given in the recipes for salads and uncooked dishes.

Herbs are used freely. If not all the named herbs are available, take those available and perhaps a substitute. For cooked dishes dried herbs are very useful if fresh ones are not available. Their flavour is rather concentrated, and as a general rule much less (say a quarter) than the given quantities is sufficient.

Oil and Lemon Dressing.

4 Tbs. oil	½ Tbs. lemon juice
a little brown sugar (optional)	

Mix the oil and lemon together well and add the sugar.

Mayonnaise (1) (Egg Mayonnaise)

2 egg yolks	2 Tbs. lemon juice
½ pt good-quality oil	salt to taste

Making mayonnaise is actually quite simple after you have had a little experience.

Keep all ingredients and the mixing bowl cool but not icy. Beat the egg yolks with a wire whisk for a short time. Then pour in the oil from a small jug for the first 5 mins. drop by drop, beating quickly all the time; then increase the flow slightly (say, to 1 tsp. at a time), but never stop whisking. When the mayonnaise starts to thicken still larger amounts of oil (1 Tbs.) can be put in at a time. When it gets really thick the lemon juice is added, which makes it thin again. Keep on whisking and add 1 Tbs. oil at a time until all the oil is in the mayonnaise, which should by now be fairly thick again.

If during the operation the mayonnaise should 'go off', that is if the oil and egg start to separate and the mixture curdles, there are a few methods to rescue it. The professional way is to add quickly a few drops of boiling water and then carry on as before whisking briskly but adding the oil slowly.

Another method is to start from scratch with one new egg yolk.

Add ¼ cup of oil drop by drop, and then carry on as before but using the curdled mayonnaise instead of oil.

NOTE. This mayonnaise will keep for a week or longer in a cool (not refrigerated) place.

Mayonnaise (2) (Soya Mayonnaise without Egg)

2 Tbs. soya flour	3 Tbs. lemon juice
6 Tbs. water	1 cup oil

Blend the soya flour and water to a paste. Add the oil, slowly at first (see previous recipe), whisking all the time. Lastly add the lemon juice.

Mayonnaise (3) (Less rich)

1 egg yolk	1 Tbs. flour
1 Tbs. lemon juice	½ cup water or stock
1 cup oil	½ oz. fat

Make a mayonnaise with the egg yolk, oil, and lemon juice (as on page 170). Melt the fat in a saucepan, add the flour, stew for one minute and add the water or stock. Boil until the mixture thickens (about 5 mins.). Cool. Then add the mayonnaise spoon by spoon to the cooked, cooled sauce, whisking all the time.

Vinaigrette

4 Tbs. oil	1 finely chopped onion
2 Tbs. vinegar	salt and pepper (optional)

Mix the vinegar and oil together with a whisk or fork, which will make it thicken slightly. Then add onion, pepper, and salt.

French Dressing

2 Tbs. olive oil	1 tsp. French mustard
1 Tbs. vinegar	salt and pepper to taste

Mix the vinegar and oil together with a whisk or fork, then add salt, pepper, and finally mustard. Mix again.

This dressing is often prepared at the table (using about half the quantities) by putting all the ingredients into a large table- or soup spoon held over the salad in case some is spilled. Whisk with a fork and then mix into the salad.

Almond Sauce

2 Tbs. ground almonds   ½ tsp. lemon juice
4–5 Tbs. thin cream   1 tsp. brown sugar (optional)

Mix the almonds and cream together to a fairly thick mixture and add the sugar. Then carefully add the lemon juice drop by drop, whisking all the time.

Apple Sauce

1 large cooking apple   1 tsp. brown sugar
1½ Tbs. mayonnaise (page 170)   1 tsp. lemon juice if sweet
2 Tbs. thin cream or milk   apple is used

Wash the apple in warm water and grate on a fine grater (leaving the peel on the apple). Mix with sugar and lemon juice. Add the cream or milk carefully, and finally the mayonnaise whisking all the time.

This should be a thick sweet-sour sauce.

Banana Sauce

2 ripe bananas   1 tsp. lemon juice
½ cup whipped cream   1 tsp. brown sugar

Peel and mash the bananas with a whisk until they turn into a thick sauce. Add the lemon juice at once to prevent discolouring. Add the sugar and lastly the whipped cream. This will make a thick sauce. If a thin sauce is required use milk or thin cream instead of whipped cream.

Chervil Sauce

1 cup Mayonnaise   ½ lemon
  (page 171, 2 or 3)   1 Tbs. chopped chervil

Mix the juice of ½ lemon into the mayonnaise (in addition to that which is already there), add a little salt and the chervil.

Chive Sauce

1 cup Mayonnaise (page 171)   1 Tbs. finely cut chives
½ lemon

Exactly as previous recipe, but with finely chopped chives instead of chervil. The chopping is most easily done with scissors.

Coconut Sauce (Hawaiian Sauce)

2 oz. desiccated coconut
1 Tbs. brown sugar
1 Tbs. lemon juice or
    1½ Tbs. orange juice

1 cup thin cream
or milk, or
coconut milk

Whip the cream (or milk) together with the fruit juice, add the desiccated coconut and sugar, whip again. The fruit juice should be added carefully so that the cream or milk will not curdle.

Cream Cheese Sauce

2 oz. curd cheese
1 tsp. cut chives

1 cup milk or thin cream
salt to taste

Rub the curd cheese through a sieve and whip together with the milk or cream. Add the chives and salt to taste. If the sauce is too thick, add more milk.

Egg Sauce

2 hard-boiled eggs
4 black olives
3 gherkins
1 small onion

1 tsp. chopped parsley
2 egg yolks
1 tsp. French mustard
1 Tbs. lemon juice

Peel the hard-boiled eggs and chop, as finely as possible, together with the gherkins and stoned olives, then add the egg yolks, the finely chopped onions and parsley, the salt, mustard, and lemon juice. Mash everything to a smooth paste which is, in fact, the finished sauce. If it is too thick, it can be thinned with a little oil or, better still, with 1 Tbs. mayonnaise.

This is a very rich sauce and only very little is needed if it is used as a salad dressing.

Fennel Sauce

1 cup Mayonnaise (No. 3 or 4)
1 tsp. lemon juice

½ Tbs. chopped fennel

Chop the fennel very finely, and mix first with the lemon juice then with the mayonnaise sauce.

Green Sauce (Frankfurter Sauce)

a few leaves of: a few sprigs of:
  spinach, sorrel, watercress   chervil, parsley, tarragon
2 cups Mayonnaise   1 Tbs. lemon juice
  (page 170 or 171)

Make a purée of all the green stuff by pouring boiling water over it (blanching) or chopping it up very finely, and then passing it through a fine sieve, and add to the mayonnaise. Finally mix in the lemon juice.

Herb Sauce

3½ Tbs. chopped fresh herbs   1 cup Mayonnaise (page 171)
  (e.g. 1 Tbs. parsley, ½ Tbs.   1 Tbs. lemon juice
  chives, 1 Tbs. tarragon, and   a little salt
  1 Tbs. chervil)

For this sauce the herbs need not be chopped as finely as in the preceding recipes. Mix them together with the lemon juice into the mayonnaise.

Horseradish Sauce

3 Tbs. mayonnaise (No. 2)   1 Tbs. lemon juice
3 Tbs. grated horseradish   1 tsp. fresh tarragon,
½ cup milk or thin cream   finely chopped

Mix the milk (or thin cream), horseradish, and tarragon together, add the lemon juice carefully and then the mayonnaise. If a thick sauce is required use ½ cup of whipped cream instead of milk.

Quite a different taste can be achieved by adding and mixing in a grated apple or ½ cup apple purée. In French cooking it is then called a Sauce Suédoise.

Mint Sauce (1)

3 Tbs. vinegar or lemon juice   1 Tbs. chopped mint
1 tsp. brown sugar   salt to taste

Mix all ingredients together.

Mint Sauce (2)

3 Tbs. mayonnaise   1 Tbs. lemon juice
   (page 170 or 171)   1 tsp. sugar
2 Tbs. chopped mint

First mix the sugar, lemon juice, and mint together, then add this to the mayonnaise.

Nut Sauce

4 oz. nuts (hazel, walnut,   1 tsp. brown sugar
   or brazil, or a mixture of   2 tsp. lemon juice
   these)
1½ cups mayonnaise (page 170)

Roast the nuts on a baking sheet in a moderate oven (300°, Reg. 4) for about 15 mins. Take them out, put them on a clean towel and rub them to get as much of the brown skin off as possible. Then grind them (coffee grinder, mincer, or liquidizer) and mix them with the lemon juice and sugar. Finally mix this into the mayonnaise.

Parsley Sauce

1 cup mayonnaise (page 170)   1 Tbs. chopped parsley
½ lemon

Exactly the same method as Chervil Sauce (page 172).

Pineapple Sauce

1 cup whipped cream   1 tsp. sugar
1 thick slice of fresh   1 tsp. lemon or orange juice
   pineapple (or 2 slices of   grated lemon rind or orange
   tinned pineapple)   rind (optional)

Chop the pineapple finely. (If a fresh pineapple is used peel it first.) Mix the chopped pineapple with the sugar, lemon juice (or orange juice), and grated peel and add the mixture carefully to the whipped cream. This is a fairly thick sauce. If a thin sauce is required use the unwhipped cream, or single cream, or milk.

Rémoulade Sauce

1 cup mayonnaise (page 171)   1 tsp. capers
2 Tbs. lemon juice   1 tsp. fresh herbs
1 hard-boiled egg   (parsley, tarragon, chives, etc.)
4 gherkins   1 tomato
4 green olives

Chop fincly: the boiled egg, gherkins, olives, capers, herbs, and tomato. Mix with the lemon juice and add to the mayonnaise.

Tartare Sauce

1 cup mayonnaise (page 171)   2 Tbs. chopped olives
2 Tbs. chopped parsley   2 Tbs. chopped gherkins
2 Tbs. chopped chives   1 tsp. chopped tarragon
2 Tbs. chopped capers   1 Tbs. lemon juice or
1 tsp. French mustard   vinegar

Mix all the ingredients, except the mayonnaise, together with the lemon juice (or vinegar), then add to the mayonnaise.

Tomato Sauce (Uncooked)

1 cup mayonnaise (page 171)   2 Tbs. sugar
1 lb. very ripe tomatoes   1 Tbs. lemon juice

Cut and sieve the tomatoes to give about 1½ cups of pulp. Mix this with the sugar and lemon juice. Finally add the mayonnaise.
   This sauce can also be used without the mayonnaise.

Vincent Sauce

This is a mixture of Tartare and Green (Frankfurter Sauce) (pages 176 and 174) in roughly equal parts.

Watercress Sauce

½ cup watercress, finely   1 cup mayonnaise (page 170)
   chopped   1 tsp. sugar
1 Tbs. lemon juice

If the watercress is very watery, strain off the water surplus. Mix the cress with the lemon juice, sugar, and perhaps a little salt, then add to the mayonnaise.

Yoghourt Sauce

1 small bottle yoghourt   1 tsp. chopped parsley
1 tsp. honey   and mint mixed

Whip the yoghourt in a mixing bowl, add the honey while whisking. Finally add the herbs.

NOTE. Yoghourt can also be used straight as a salad dressing without any addition.

UNCOOKED SALADS

Quantities

With one or two exceptions the quantities given are for one person, taking into account that an uncooked main dish normally consists of three different salads.

Apple and Date Salad. For 1

1 medium apple   1 Tbs. milk or cream
6 stoned dates   1 tsp. lemon juice
1 tsp. brown sugar

Wash the apple thoroughly, and peel it if it is suspected that any chemical or wax sprays have not been washed off. Wash the dates in warm water. Cut the apple, first into quarters then into thin slices; halve the dates and then cut them with a sharp knife also into thin slices. Mix the sugar, lemon juice, and cream (or milk) together into the salad.

Beetroot with Apple. For 1

1 small raw beetroot   1 Tbs. Oil and Lemon
1 medium cooking apple   Dressing (page 170)
1 tsp. sugar

Peel the beetroot and grate it finely. Do the same with the apple, with its core, and, if desired, with the peel. Mix the beetroot and apple together, adding the sugar as well as the oil and lemon dressing.

Beetroot with Horseradish Sauce. For 1

As in the previous recipe with the addition of 1 Tbs. Horseradish Sauce (page 174).

Beetroot with Watercress. For 1

1 small raw beetroot	1 tsp. sugar
1 Tbs. Oil and Lemon Dressing (page 170)	2 Tbs. chopped watercress

As for Beetroot with Apple above, but with the chopped watercress instead of the apple.

Beetroot with Raisins. For 1

1 small raw beetroot	1 tsp. sugar
1 Tbs. Oil and Lemon Dressing (page 170)	½ oz. raisins

As for Beetroot with Apple, but with 6 oz. washed and stoned raisins instead of the apple.

Cabbage Mayonnaise. For 1

3 oz. green cabbage	1½ Tbs. mayonnaise
½ tsp. sugar	(No. 1, 2, or 3)

After cleaning shred the cabbage. Add the sugar and mix with the mayonnaise.

Cabbage with Raisins. For 1

3 oz. green cabbage	1½ Tbs. mayonnaise
½ oz. raisins	(No. 1, 2, or 3)

As in the previous recipe but with the addition of the washed and stoned raisins, mixed into the cabbage.

Cabbage with Apple Sauce. For 1

3 oz. green cabbage	1 Tbs. Oil and Lemon
½ tsp. sugar	Dressing (page 170)
1½ Tbs. Apple Sauce (page 172)	

Prepare the cabbage as for Cabbage Mayonnaise above, but

dress with oil and lemon instead of mayonnaise. Top with the apple sauce.

Carrots

All carrots should be washed and peeled. Uncooked carrots taste sweeter and juicier the finer they are grated. But use any grater you like, according to taste and convenience.

Carrot Mayonnaise. For 1

1 medium carrot	1 Tbs. mayonnaise
1 tsp. sugar (optional)	(page 170 or 171)

Grate the carrot, add the sugar if desired, and mix with the mayonnaise.

Carrot with Coconut. For 1

1 medium carrot	1 Tbs. Coconut Sauce
1 tsp. sugar (optional)	(page 173)

Shred carrots finely and mix with the sugar (optional) and the coconut sauce.

Carrot with Banana. For 1

1 medium carrot	1 tsp. lemon juice
½ banana	1 Tbs. cream or milk
1 tsp. sugar	

Shred the carrot. Cut the banana lengthwise and then in thin slices across. Mix the lemon juice, cream, and sugar together, then mix the carrot and banana into it.

Carrot and Apple. For 1

1 medium carrot	1 tsp. cream or milk
1 small eating apple	½ tsp. sugar
1 tsp. lemon juice	

Shred the carrot and apple coarsely or finely but both in the same way. Then mix all ingredients together.

Carrot with Grated Cheese

1 medium carrot	1 Tbs. Oil and Lemon
2 Tbs. grated cheese	Dressing (page 170)

Shred the carrot and mix with the dressing and 1 Tbs. grated cheese. Top with the rest of the grated cheese.

Carrot and Celery. For 1

1 medium carrot	1 Tbs. mayonnaise
2 or 3 small pieces celery	(No. 1, 2, or 3)

Shred the carrot coarsely and cut the celery into small cubes. Mix with the mayonnaise.

Carrot Pudding. For 2

1 medium carrot	1 tsp. lemon juice
1 Tbs. grated nuts	1 tsp. mixed herbs
1 Tbs. oats or cornflakes	(parsley, chives, tarragon)
2 Tbs. milk	

Soak the flakes in the milk and add the grated nuts, lemon juice, and chopped herbs. Add the very finely grated carrot, mix and then let it stand for about $\frac{1}{2}$ hour. The mixture should then be firm enough to be formed into a pudding shape. If it is too thin add a few oats or cornflakes. Specially tasty with Nut Sauce (page 175).

Carrots with Chive Sauce. For 1

1 medium carrot	1 Tbs. Oil and Lemon
1 Tbs. Chive Sauce (page 172)	Dressing (page 170)

Mix the grated carrots with the dressing and top with the chive sauce.

Carrots, Figs, and Apples. For 2

1 medium carrot	1 Tbs. ground almonds
1 medium apple	2 Tbs. cream
3 or 4 dried figs	2 tsp. lemon juice

Cut the carrot and apple into cubes and the figs in half and put them all through a mincer. Then add the ground almonds, lemon juice, and 1 tsp. brown sugar (optional). Mix well together. Can be served with Apple Sauce (page 172) or, with whipped cream, as a sweet.

Cauliflower

Washing and soaking in salt water is important because of insects. For the following recipes the cauliflower should be cut or shredded on a very coarse grater, never finely.

Cauliflower with Herb Mayonnaise. For 1

3 oz. cauliflower
1½ Tbs. Herb Sauce (page 174)

Mix the shredded or cut cauliflower with the herb sauce and serve immediately as cauliflower discolours quickly.

Cauliflower with Nuts. For 1

2 oz. cauliflower   1 Tbs. mayonnaise (page 170)
1 oz. nuts, any kind

Cut the nuts into small pieces (about the size of a quarter hazelnut) and mix with the shredded cauliflower and the mayonnaise.

Cauliflower and Carrots. For 1

2 oz. cauliflower   ½ small onion
1 small carrot   1 Tbs. mayonnaise (page 170)
½ tsp. sugar

Shred the cauliflower and carrot on a coarse grater, chop the onion finely, and mix with the sugar and mayonnaise.

Cauliflower and Tomato. For 1

2 oz. cauliflower   1 tsp. chopped chives
1 tomato   1 tsp. chopped parsley
1 Tbs. mayonnaise (page 170)

Cut the tomato into small cubes, mix with the chives, parsley, and mayonnaise, and lastly with the shredded cauliflower.

Celery Mayonnaise. For 1

2 or 3 pieces of celery (white inside pieces)
½ tsp. lemon juice   1 Tbs. mayonnaise
½ tsp. sugar   (page 170 or 171)

Chop the celery finely (you will need a very sharp knife), and mix it with the lemon juice, sugar, and mayonnaise.

Celery and Apple. For 1

2 pieces celery   ½ tsp. lemon juice
1 medium apple*   1 Tbs. cream or milk
1 tsp. sugar

Wash the apple in warm water, quarter it, take out the core and cut the apple into small cubes. Then mix it with the sliced celery, cream, sugar, and lemon juice.

Celery and Dates. For 1

2 pieces celery   1 Tbs. yoghourt or Yoghourt
3 or 4 stoned dates   Sauce (page 177)

Cut the celery and dates into small pieces and mix them with the yoghourt or yoghourt sauce.

Celery Rémoulade. For 1

3 pieces celery   1 Tbs. Rémoulade Sauce
                                  (page 176)

Mix the sliced celery into the rémoulade sauce.

Celery and Tomato. For 1

2 pieces celery   1 tsp. chopped tarragon and
1 tomato   chives mixed
½ tsp. lemon juice   1 Tbs. mayonnaise (page 171)

Cut the celery and tomato into small pieces, mix with the herbs, lemon juice, and mayonnaise.

* A sweet-sour apple is best; if only sweet dessert apples are available double the quantity of lemon juice.

Celery and Carrot. For 1

2 pieces celery	½ tsp. lemon juice
1 small carrot	½ tsp. chopped parsley
½ tsp. brown sugar	1 Tbs. yoghourt

Cut the celery into small pieces, grate the carrot on a coarse grater. Mix together with lemon juice, sugar, parsley, and yoghourt.

Celeriac Mayonnaise. For 1

½ medium celeriac	1 tsp. chopped chives and/or
½ tsp. lemon juice	parsley
½ tsp. sugar	1 Tbs. mayonnaise
1 tsp. oil	(No. 1, 2, or 3)

Peel the celeriac and shred on a coarse grater. Mix with the herb(s), lemon juice, oil, and sugar. Then mix in the mayonnaise. If the celeriac is very dry add 1 Tbs. milk before mixing in the mayonnaise.

Celeriac Rémoulade. For 1

½ medium celeriac	1½ Tbs. Rémoulade Sauce
½ tsp. lemon juice	(page 176)

Shred the celeriac on a coarse grater and mix with the lemon juice and rémoulade sauce.

Celeriac with Dates. For 1

½ medium celeriac	1 tsp. grated nuts
4 stoned dried dates	1½ Tbs. Yoghourt Sauce
	(page 177)

Shred the celeriac coarsely and cut the dates into small pieces. Mix the celeriac and dates with the yoghourt sauce and top with grated nuts.

Chicory Mayonnaise. For 1

1 medium stick chicory	1 Tbs. mayonnaise
½ small onion	(No. 1, 2, or 3)
1 tsp. lemon juice	1 tsp. chopped parsley

Cut the washed chicory lengthwise in half, then across into thin slices, and mix it immediately with the lemon juice (to prevent discolouring). Chop the onion finely, mix first with the chopped parsley, and then with the other ingredients.

Chicory Rémoulade. For 1

Exactly as in the previous recipe but with Rémoulade Sauce (page 176) instead of the mayonnaise.

Chicory and Tomato. For 1

1 small stick chicory	1 Tbs. mayonnaise
1 medium tomato	(page 170 or 171)
1 tsp. lemon juice	1 tsp. chopped herbs
½ tsp. sugar	(chives and parsley)

Cut the chicory and mix with lemon juice as for Chicory Mayonnaise. Cut the tomato into small cubes and mix all the ingredients together.

Chicory and Orange. For 1

1 small stick chicory	1 tsp. sugar or honey
½ medium orange	1 Tbs. yoghourt or cream

Cut the peeled orange into very small pieces, cut the chicory as for Chicory Mayonnaise and mix at once with the orange, then with the other ingredients.

Filled Chicory. For 2 or 3

1 stick chicory	2 tsp. chopped herbs (chives,
1½ Tbs. cream cheese	parsley, and tarragon)
1 Tbs. cream or milk	2 slices of tomato

Wash the chicory and separate the outer leaves carefully, as they are to be used as the outer shells of boatshaped dishes. Make the filling (for 4 to 6 boats) by whipping the cream cheese together with the cream (or milk), and mixing in the chopped herbs and one chopped up slice of tomato. This mixture is then piled into the outer leaves of the chicory and topped with strips of tomato as decoration.

Cole Slaw. For 1

2 oz. white cabbage	1 tsp. tomato purée
¼ small pepper	1½ Tbs. Oil and Lemon
1 medium carrot	Dressing or Vinaigrette
½ tsp. brown sugar	(pages 170 and 171)
½ small onion	

Shred or slice the cabbage as for Cabbage Mayonnaise (page 178), shred the carrots finely, chop the onion and pepper (the fleshy outer skin only). Then add the tomato purée and the dressing and finally mix all ingredients well together.

Corn Salad (Lamb's Lettuce)

This is a very useful plant because it is available during autumn and winter when other green salads are scarce. It has, unfortunately, gone somewhat out of use. Its lancet-shaped leaves are prepared and used like lettuce.

Cucumber Salad. For 1

3-in. piece cucumber	1½ Tbs. yoghourt
1 tsp. mixed herbs	½ tsp. sugar
1 tsp. chives	a little salt (optional)
1 tsp. lemon juice	

Cut the cucumber (peeled) into very thin slices. Mix lemon juice, finely chopped herbs, chives, sugar, and yoghourt together and pour this dressing over the cucumber.

Cucumber and Tomatoes. For 1

2-in. piece cucumber	1 tsp. lemon juice
1 medium tomato	½ tsp. sugar
1 tsp. chopped chives	1 Tbs. mayonnaise (page 171)

Cut the cucumber and tomato into thin slices and mix well with the other ingredients.

Cucumber, Tomato, and Spring Onions (Salade May Irwin). For 1

2-in. piece cucumber	1 tsp. lemon juice
1 medium tomato	½ tsp. sugar
2 spring onions	1 Tbs. mayonnaise
salt to taste	(page 170 or 171)

Cut the tomato into 8 pieces and the cucumber into pieces of roughly the same size. Cut the spring onions fairly finely and mix all ingredients together.

Filled Cucumber. For 2

6-in. piece cucumber	1 tsp. chopped herbs
½ small tomato	(parsley and chives)
2 tsp. oats	1 Tbs. milk
1 tsp. grated nuts	1 tsp. lemon juice
1 Tbs. mayonnaise (page 170)	

Cut the cucumber across into 4 pieces, core out the soft inside and chop this finely. Mix it with the oats and milk and let stand for about 10 mins. Then add the herbs, the lemon juice, the tomato (chopped), and the mayonnaise and mix to a stiff mixture. If it is runny add a few more oats. Fill the mixture back into the cored-out cucumber rings and top with grated nuts.

Dandelion Salad. For 1

3 oz. young dandelion leaves	1 tsp. lemon juice
1 Tbs. mayonnaise (page 170)	½ tsp. sugar

Wash the leaves carefully. If they are large tear them into smaller pieces (do not cut as this may spoil the colour). Mix with the sugar, lemon juice, and mayonnaise.

NOTE. Oil and Lemon Dressing (page 170) or Vinaigrette (page 171) can be used instead of lemon juice and mayonnaise.

Endive Salad. For 4

1 head endive	1 Tbs. French Dressing or
1 onion (chopped)	Oil and Lemon Dressing
1 tsp. mixed herbs	

Trim off the root of the endive and the brown outer leaves (if any). Divide it into its single leaves and wash carefully several times, at least once under running water. Drain and cut the leaves into small (1-inch) pieces. Wash again and drain well or better still shake it dry in a colander. Mix well with the herbs and the dressing. The salad will improve if left standing for ½ hour.

Fennel Mayonnaise. For 1

½ small fennel	1 Tbs. mayonnaise (No. 1, 2, or 3)
½ tsp. chopped onion	1 tsp. lemon juice

Wash the fennel and cut it first in quarters, then in thin slices. Then mix all the ingredients together.

Fennel and Tomato. For 1

As previous recipe but with the addition of a small tomato cut into small cubes.

Fennel and Apple. For 1

¼ fennel	½ tsp. lemon juice
1 medium apple	1 tsp. sugar
1½ Tbs. cream	salt to taste

Cut the fennel into thin slices. Core the apple and shred on a coarse grater. Mix the cream, lemon juice, and sugar together and mix with the fennel and apple.

Fennel, Tomato, and Pepper. For 1

¼ fennel	1 tsp. chopped onion or
1 medium tomato	chives
¼ small pepper	1 Tbs. mayonnaise (No. 1, 2, or 3)
1 tsp. lemon juice	salt to taste

Cut the fennel into thin slices, and the tomato and pepper (the outer fleshy skin only) into small cubes. Then mix all the ingredients together.

Kohlrabi Mayonnaise. For 1

1 large kohlrabi*	½ tsp. sugar
1 tsp. lemon juice	salt to taste
1 Tbs. mayonnaise (page 170)	

Peel the kohlrabi, cut it first in quarters, then in thin slices. Alternatively shred it on a coarse grater. Mix all the ingredients together.

Kohlrabi and Carrot. For 1

1 medium kohlrabi*	1 Tbs. mayonnaise (No. 1, 2, or 3)
1 small carrot	½ tsp. brown sugar
1 tsp. lemon juice	1 tsp. chopped parsley

After peeling the kohlrabi and carrot, shred them on a coarse grater. Mix all the ingredients together.

Kohlrabi with Herb Sauce. For 1

1 large kohlrabi*	1 Tbs. Herb Sauce (page 174)
½ Tbs. oil	1 tsp. lemon juice
½ tsp. sugar	salt to taste

Peel the kohlrabi and shred it on a coarse grater. Mix the lemon juice and oil together, mix in the kohlrabi, and top with the herb sauce.

Leek, Tomato, and Apple. For 1

½ leek (the white part only)	1 tsp. lemon juice
1 small cooking apple	½ tsp. sugar
1 small tomato	1 Tbs. mayonnaise (No. 1, 2, or 3)

After washing it cut the leek first lengthwise in half, then across into thin slices. Wash or peel the apple, cut it in quarters and remove the core. Cut the apple and tomato in small cubes. Then mix all ingredients together.

* The tuberous part only, not the leaves.

Lettuce with Lemon Dressing. For 1

½ small lettuce	1 Tbs. Oil and Lemon Dressing
½ tsp. sugar	a little salt to taste

Use all the sound lettuce leaves (not only the inside ones). Wash them carefully at least once under running water. Drain (this is most easily done in a wire basket), and shake until the water has disappeared. If necessary dry on a towel. The leaves can be torn or broken into small pieces but should never be cut as this bruises them. Mix the dressing with the sugar, pour it over the lettuce, and mix well.

Lettuce with French Dressing. For 1

As in the previous recipe but with French Dressing (page 171) instead of Oil and Lemon Dressing. Do not include sugar, but add perhaps a little salt.

Lettuce Salad, Hungarian Style. For 2

½ small lettuce	1½ Tbs. French Dressing
1 small tomato	(page 171)
2-in. piece of cucumber	salt to taste
¼ pepper	a little cayenne pepper
⅓ small onion	

After washing and drying the lettuce leaves, break them in fairly small pieces. Slice the tomato and cucumber; chop the onion and pepper (fleshy outer skin only). Mix all the ingredients, including the dressing, together.

Marrow Mayonnaise. For 1

½ small marrow*	1 Tbs. mayonnaise (No. 1, 2, or 3)
1 tsp. sugar	2 tsp. mixed herbs
1 tsp. lemon juice	(chives, parsley, tarragon,
salt to taste	chervil)

Peel the marrow and remove the pulp. Shred on a coarse grater. Mix all ingredients together.

* Courgettes may be treated in the same way as marrows.

Marrow and Tomato. For 1

The same as the previous recipe, but with the addition of one cubed tomato.

Marrow Rémoulade. For 1

As for Marrow Mayonnaise with 1 Tbs. Rémoulade Sauce (page 176) instead of the mayonnaise.

Macédoine of Vegetables. For 3

1 small carrot	1 small tomato
1 piece celery or celeriac	1 medium apple
½ small turnip or parsnip	2-in. piece cucumber or
1 Tbs. chopped leeks	marrow
1 small chopped onion	2 green olives
1 tsp. chopped parsley	3 or 4 capers
2 Tbs. mayonnaise	½ tsp. lemon juice
(No. 1, 2, or 3)	2 tsp. sugar
2 sprigs cauliflower	salt to taste

After washing cut all the vegetables, except the cauliflower and the chopped items, into small cubes. The smaller and the more neatly the cubes are cut the more attractive the salad will look. The cauliflower is cut into thin slices. Chop the olives and capers, mix with the chopped leeks, onion, and parsley, then mix all cubed vegetables. The chopped items are separately mixed with the lemon juice and mayonnaise, this is poured over the mixed vegetables and the salad carefully turned over (in order not to break up the vegetables) and mixed.

Mixed Root Mayonnaise. For 2

1 small carrot	½ small chopped onion
½ parsnip	1 tsp. sugar
½ turnip or swede	1 tsp. chopped parsley
1 small beetroot (raw)	2 Tbs. lemon juice
2 Tbs. oil	salt to taste

Grate all the vegetables finely and mix them together. Then make a dressing of the lemon juice, sugar, oil, parsley, and onion. Pour it over the vegetables and mix again.

NOTE. The selection and combination of root vegetables can of course be changed according to taste and availability. A more interesting flavour can be achieved by the addition of 1 Tbs. currants or raisins.

Parsnip Mayonnaise. For 1

½ medium parsnip	½ tsp. chopped parsley
½ tsp. sugar	1 Tbs. mayonnaise (No. 1, 2, or 3)

Peel the parsnip and grate finely, add the sugar, parsley, and mayonnaise and mix.

Parsnip and Dates. For 1

½ small parsnip	1 tsp. sugar
4–6 dates	1½ Tbs. yoghourt or
1 tsp. lemon juice	cream

Cut the dates into small pieces and mix with the finely shredded parsnip. Make a dressing of the yoghourt (or cream), sugar, and lemon juice and mix this with the parsnips and dates.

Pumpkin with Apples. For 1

3 oz. pumpkin (peeled)	1 tsp. lemon juice
1 medium apple (cooking	1 tsp. sugar
or sharp dessert)	1 tsp. grated nuts
1 Tbs. cream	

Shred the pumpkin on a coarse grater, the apple on a fine one. Make a dressing of cream, lemon juice, and sugar and mix with the pumpkin and apple. Top with grated nuts.

NOTE. A variation is to leave out the apple but top with Apple Sauce (page 172) and the grated nuts.

Radish Salad with Herb Sauce. For 1

6–8 large radishes*	2 tsp. oil
1 tsp. lemon juice	sugar and salt to taste
1 Tbs. Herb Sauce (page 174)	

Top and tail the radishes, wash them and cut them into thin

* Equivalent amount of black radish can be used.

slices. Mix with the lemon juice, oil, and sugar. Top with herb sauce.

Red Cabbage Salad. For 1

2–3 oz. red cabbage	1 tsp. lemon juice
½ medium apple	1 tsp. sugar
1 Tbs. oil	salt (optional)

Shred the cabbage on a coarse grater or slice finely. Grate the apple finely. Mix the red cabbage, apple, lemon juice, oil, and sugar well together. As this salad needs some time for blending, let it stand for ½ hour before serving.

Red Cabbage Salad with Various Sauces. For 1

The Red Cabbage Salad (previous recipe) is also excellent with 1½ Tbs. of one of the following sauces poured over it: Apple Sauce (page 172); Nut Sauce (page 175); Horseradish Sauce (page 174).

Sauerkraut Salad. For 4

6 oz. sauerkraut	2 Tbs. mayonnaise
1 large apple	(No. 1, 2, or 3)
1 tsp. chopped parsley	1 tsp. sugar

Sauerkraut is available in tins or loose from barrels. The latter type is preferable for salads (home-made is better still). Wash the sauerkraut and strain. Cut the apple into small pieces and mix all the ingredients together. The addition of salt is optional.

Chopped onions, spring onions, and herbs can be used instead of the apple.

Spinach Mayonnaise. For 1

2 oz. fresh spinach	a little salt and/or sugar
1 tsp. lemon juice	is optional according to taste
1 Tbs. mayonnaise (page 171)	

The washed spinach should be well drained (perhaps shaken in a wire basket or dried on a towel) and chopped very finely. Only fresh leaves should be used, not the stems. Squeeze out any surplus water and mix with all the other ingredients.

Spinach and Tomato. For 1

2 oz. spinach	1 tsp. lemon juice
1 medium tomato	1 Tbs. mayonnaise (No. 1, 2, or 3)

Exactly as previous recipe but with the addition of finely cubed tomato.

Spinach with Nuts. For 1

2 oz. spinach	1 Tbs. mayonnaise
1 tsp. lemon juice	(No. 1, 2, or 3)
½ tsp. sugar	1 oz. grated nuts

As for Spinach Mayonnaise. Finish by mixing in the nuts, which should be coarsely grated.

Spinach Pudding. For 1

1½ oz. spinach	1 Tbs. grated cheese
1½ Tbs. oats or cornflakes	1 tsp. grated nuts or almonds
1 tsp. lemon juice	2 Tbs. milk

Prepare the spinach and drain as for Spinach Mayonnaise. Soak the oats or cornflakes in the milk (10 to 15 mins.), add to the spinach and mix all ingredients together; the result should be a fairly thick mixture. Press this into a cup or small pudding basin and turn out on a plate. Specially attractive if served with Tomato Sauce (page 176).

Swede Mayonnaise. For 1

2 oz. swedes	1 Tbs. mayonnaise
1 tsp. lemon juice	(No. 1, 2, or 3)
1 tsp. sugar	

Shred the peeled swedes on a fine grater and mix all ingredients together.

Swedes with Spring Onions

Exactly as the previous recipe but with the addition of 2 or 3 finely cut spring onions.

Swedes and Carrots. For 1

1½ oz. swedes   1 Tbs. mayonnaise
1 medium carrot   (No. 1, 2, or 3)
1 tsp. lemon juice   1 tsp. sugar

The peeled swedes and carrots are finely grated and mixed with all the other ingredients.

Turnip Mayonnaise. For 1

1 medium turnip   1 Tbs. mayonnaise
1 tsp. lemon juice   (No. 1, 2, or 3)
1 tsp. sugar   1 tsp. chopped parsley

Peel the turnip and grate finely, then mix all the ingredients together.

Turnips and Dates. For 1

1 small turnip   1 Tbs. cream or milk
6 stoned dates   1 tsp. lemon juice
1½ tsp. sugar

Peel the turnip and grate it finely. Cut the dates into small pieces and mix all the ingredients together.

Tomato Salad. For 1

2 medium tomatoes   1 Tbs. oil
1 tsp. chives   a little sugar and/or
1 tsp. lemon juice   salt (optional)

Make a mixture of the chives (chopped onions or spring onions can be used instead), lemon juice, oil, and sugar and pour over the sliced tomatoes. Mix carefully to avoid damaging the slices.

Tomato Mayonnaise. For 1

As previous recipe but with mayonnaise instead of oil.

Tomatoes with Cream Cheese. For 1

As Tomato Salad but with Cream Cheese Sauce (page 173) instead of oil.

Tomatoes aux Fines Herbes. For 1

As Tomato Salad but with Herb Sauce (page 174) instead of oil.

Filled Tomato (1) (with Cream Cheese). For 1

2 medium tomatoes	1 tsp. chives and parsley mixed
1 tsp. mayonnaise	½ tsp. lemon juice
2 tsp. cream cheese	salt to taste
1 tsp. milk or cream	

Cut the tops off the tomatoes (keep them as lids). Scoop out the insides and mix this with the other ingredients. Then use this mixture to fill the tomatoes, and put the lids back on. Decorate with a little parsley and/or by piping a little mayonnaise on top.

Filled Tomato (2). For 1

2 medium tomatoes	½ Tbs. mayonnaise
1 Tbs. oats or cornflakes	½ tsp. chopped onions
½ Tbs. milk	½ tsp. chopped parsley
½ tsp. lemon juice	salt to taste

Prepare the tomatoes as in the previous recipe. Make the filling by soaking the flakes in milk for 10 to 15 mins. and mixing this with the inside of the tomato and the other ingredients. Stuff the filling back into the tomatoes and put the lids on top.

Tomatoes and Cucumber. For 1

2 medium tomatoes	1 tsp. lemon juice
1-in. piece cucumber	½ tsp. sugar
1 tsp. chopped chives	1 Tbs. mayonnaise

Cut the tomatoes and cucumber into thin slices and mix with the other ingredients.

FRUIT SALADS AS PART OF AN UNCOOKED MAIN DISH

American Salad. For 4

2 medium dessert apples	1 Tbs. sugar
1 large orange	2 Tbs. water
1 grapefruit	1 Tbs. whipped cream
2 or 3 medium tomatoes	(optional)

After washing the fruit cut the apples and tomatoes into thick (½-inch) pieces, and divide the orange and grapefruit into segments and halve these. Mix the fruit (including the tomatoes) with the sugar and water, serve on a bed of lettuce and, if desired, top with whipped cream.

Florida Salad. For 4

2 medium dessert apples	1 Tbs. sugar
2 medium oranges	2 to 3 Tbs. water
1 grapefruit	1 Tbs. curd cheese or
3 medium tomatoes	cream cheese

Prepare as in the previous recipe and top with cream cheese.

Grapefruit Salad. For 4

2 grapefruits	1–2 Tbs. sugar
1 orange	2 Tbs. water
2 apples	1 Tbs. whipped cream
2 tomatoes	

Prepare exactly as American Salad above.

Pineapple Salad. For 4

2 thick slices pineapple	1 tomato
2 medium dessert apples	1 Tbs. sugar
1 orange	2–3 Tbs. water
1 grapefruit	1 Tbs. whipped cream (optional)

Prepare the fruit, including the tomato, as for American Salad, and cut the pineapple in ½-inch pieces. Top with whipped cream and a few pieces of pineapple as decoration.

Specially attractive if Pineapple Sauce (page 175) is used instead of cream.

Grape Salad. For 4

½ lb. ripe grapes	1 Tbs. water
2 apples	1 Tbs. whipped cream
2 oranges	1 tsp. grated nuts
1 Tbs. sugar	a few cherries (glacé or fresh)

Wash the grapes thoroughly in water to which a small amount of vinegar has been added. Drain and cut each grape in half, removing the pips. Cut the cherries in half and remove stones (if fresh cherries). The other fruit is prepared as for American Salad. Mix all the fruit together with the sugar and water. Serve on a bed of lettuce, topped with cream and grated nuts.

Mixed Cherry Salad. For 4

½ lb. ripe cherries	1 Tbs. sugar
¼ lb. grapes (optional)	3 Tbs. water
1 orange	1 Tbs. whipped cream
3 apples	

Wash and stone the cherries. If they are small, leave them whole after stoning; otherwise cut them in half. Prepare the grapes as in the previous salad, the other fruit as for American Salad. Keep a few cherries back for decoration. Mix the fruit with sugar and water and serve the salad on a bed of lettuce. Top with the whipped cream and a few cherries.

Kentucky Salad. For 4

3 large soft pears	1 Tbs. sugar
¼ lb. cherries	2 Tbs. water
1 orange	1 Tbs. whipped cream
2 apples	1 tsp. grated nuts
2 tomatoes	

Peel and quarter the pears, then cut them into ½-inch pieces. Stone the cherries and cut up all the other fruit as for American Salad. Serve on a bed of lettuce, topped with whipped cream and grated nuts.

Salade Mimosa. For 4

¼ lb. corn salad	2 Tbs. Oil and Lemon Dressing
4 medium tangerines	(page 170)
1 hard-boiled egg	

Cut the roots off the corn salad and remove any brown leaves. Wash them thoroughly. Peel the tangerines and separate the segments. Peel the egg and chop it finely. Now drain the corn salad well (shaking in wire basket is a good method), and mix with the oil and lemon dressing. Line a salad bowl or plate with the corn salad, decorate with the tangerines and sprinkle the chopped egg over the lot.

Waldorf Salad. For 4

1 head celery or	8 stoned dates
1 medium celeriac	2 tsp. lemon juice
1 large apple	2 tsp. sugar
2 bananas	2 Tbs. mayonnaise
¼ lb. walnut kernels	(No. 1, 2, or 3)

Cut the washed celery into small pieces. (The celeriac should be shredded on a coarse grater.) Cut (or grate) the apple and bananas into pieces of a similar size. Cut the walnuts and dates in halves or quarters. Mix everything together, first the fruit and then the other ingredients.

SALADS MADE WITH COOKED INGREDIENTS

Asparagus Salad. For 4

1 lb. asparagus or a large tin	3 Tbs. Vinaigrette (page 171)

Cook the asparagus (see page 45), and drain and cool it. Arrange it on a plate and pour the vinaigrette over the tips.

Mayonnaise (1, 2, or 3, page 170 or 171) can be used instead of Vinaigrette. This is then often served separately.

Aubergine Salad. For 4

2 good-sized aubergines or 3 small ones	1 small onion
3 Tbs. Vinaigrette (page 171)	1 tsp. chopped parsley

Boil the aubergines (see page 74) until they are fairly soft. Drain and cut them in half lengthwise. Take off the skin (which is discarded) and cut the inside into small pieces. Mix the chopped onion with the vinaigrette and parsley, then pour this over the aubergine pieces.

Avocado Pear Salad. For 4

2 avocado pears (ripe, uncooked)
2 hard-boiled eggs
1 tomato
1 Tbs. oats
1 tsp. parsley chopped
1 tsp. chives
3 Tbs. mayonnaise (page 171)
salt to taste

Wash the avocado pears and cut them in half lengthwise; remove the stone. Chop the eggs finely and mix them with the oats, parsley, and chives. Cut the tomato into very small cubes and add these to the egg mixture. Add the mayonnaise. This should now be a fairly thick sauce which is heaped on the avocado halves. Serve on a bed of lettuce and decorate with a tomato slice.

Beetroot Salad. For 4

1 large cooked beetroot
1 medium onion
1 Tbs. sugar
2 Tbs. vinegar
1 Tbs. tepid water
½ tsp. caraway seed (optional)
½ tsp. salt (optional)

Peel the beetroot and cut it into thin slices. Peel the onion and cut it into rings. Now make a dressing from the water, sugar, and vinegar to which, if desired, the caraway seed and salt can be added. Mix this dressing carefully (in order not to break the beetroot slices) with the onions and beetroots.

French Bean Salad. For 4

1 lb. French beans
1 small onion
1 tsp. chopped parsley
1 tsp. chopped chives
1 tsp. sugar
1½ Tbs. vinegar
3 Tbs. oil
salt to taste

Top, tail, and wash the beans. Break or cut them into pieces about 1 inch long and boil them in very little water until they are soft. Strain and let them cool. Chop the onion and add it to the beans. Now make a dressing from all the other ingredients and mix well with the beans.

This salad should be prepared a few hours before being served.

Salade Carmen. For 4

1 large cooked beetroot	1 tsp. sugar
½ head of raw celery	2 Tbs. vinegar
1 small onion chopped	3 Tbs. oil

Peel the beetroot and cut it into strips about ½ inch square and 2 inches long. Clean the celery carefully and cut it into similar strips. Mix both together. Make a dressing from all the other ingredients, pour over the beetroot and celery, and mix.

Bohemian Salad. For 4

4 cooked potatoes	2 large tomatoes
1 medium cooked carrot	1 small chopped onion
2 Tbs. cooked peas	1 tsp. chopped herbs
½ apple	(parsley and tarragon)
2 Tbs. vinegar	3 Tbs. mayonnaise (page 170)
1 Tbs. warm milk or water	salt to taste

Cut the carrot, tomatoes, and apple into very small cubes, and the potatoes into somewhat larger cubes. Mix these ingredients together with the peas. Pour the warm water (or milk) over the vegetables and let them stand for 15 mins. In the meantime mix the chopped onion with the rest of the ingredients and pour over the vegetables. Mix well.

This salad should be prepared one or two hours before being served.

Cauliflower Salad. For 4

1 medium cauliflower	1 Tbs. vinegar
2 tsp. chopped herbs	3 Tbs. oil
(parsley, chives, chervil)	salt optional

Divide the cauliflower into sprigs and wash it carefully. Boil it in a little water until it is fairly soft, with the sprigs still intact. Strain but keep 2 Tbs. of the cauliflower water for the dressing. This is made by mixing this water with the vinegar, oil, herbs, and salt. Pour it over the cooled cauliflower and mix slightly but very carefully (preferably with a silver spoon), in order not to break the sprigs.

This salad should be prepared one or two hours before being served.

Celeriac Salad. For 4

1 large celeriac   4 Tbs. Vinaigrette (page 171)
1 tsp. chopped parsley

Cook the celeriac whole until it is fairly soft. Take it out of the water, cool it a little, and peel it. Then cut it in slices, but not too thin (it breaks easily). Sprinkle the chopped parsley over it and mix in the vinaigrette carefully, preferably with a silver spoon. It should be prepared an hour before being served.

Salade Créole. For 4

3 Tbs. cooked peas   1 tsp. sugar
3 oz. rice   2 tsp. chopped parsley
2 tomatoes   1 Tbs. vinegar
½ small sweet pepper   3 Tbs. mayonnaise
1 medium onion   ½ tsp. salt (optional)

Cook the rice (see page 123). Cut the tomatoes into small cubes and chop the pepper and onion finely. Mix together: cooked rice, peas, tomatoes, pepper, onion, and parsley. Make a dressing from the sugar, vinegar, and mayonnaise (and salt if desired) and mix it into the vegetables.

Egg Salad. For 4

4 hard-boiled eggs   1 Tbs. vinegar
1 tomato   4 Tbs. mayonnaise (No. 1, 2, or 3)
2 spring onions   some radishes for garnish
1 tsp. chopped parsley   salt to taste
1 Tbs. milk

Shell the eggs and cut them and the tomatoes in slices. Make a dressing by mixing the chopped spring onions, parsley, vinegar, milk, salt, and lastly the mayonnaise. Mix this with the egg and tomato slices and garnish with radishes.

Italian Salad. For 4

1 lb. root vegetables cooked
(such as carrots, parsnips,
turnips, but *no* beetroots)
1 large apple
½ raw leek
2 Tbs. cooked peas
3–4 Tbs. mayonnaise

2 Tbs. cooked white haricot
beans
3 gherkins
1 tsp. chopped chives and
parsley
2 Tbs. vinegar
salt to taste

Cut the root vegetables and the apple into small cubes, neatly
and evenly, and the leeks into small pieces. Chop the gherkins
finely, mix the remaining ingredients, and pour this dressing
over the salad. Mix well. This salad can be served immediately
or stand for an hour or two.

Salade Lorette. For 4

4 oz. corn salad
1 medium cooked celeriac
2 medium cooked beetroots

4 Tbs. Oil and Lemon Dressing
or French Dressing

Cut the peeled beetroots and celeriac into strips about one inch
long. Mix them with the dressing and serve on a bed of corn
salad (see page 185). If no corn salad is available lettuce will do as
second best.

Continental Potato Salad. For 4

1 lb. cooked potatoes
3 gherkins
1 tsp. capers
1 tsp. chives
1 tsp. parsley and/or
tarragon
½ cup sour milk or yoghourt

1 small onion
½ cup hot water
3 Tbs. vinegar
2 Tbs. oil
1 tsp. sugar
4 Tbs. mayonnaise (No. 1, 2, or 3)

Waxy potatoes are best for potato salad, as the floury kind break
too easily. Cut the peeled potatoes into thin slices. Chop the
onion, gherkin, capers, tarragon, and parsley finely; the chives
are better cut separately. Pour the hot water over the potato
slices and let them stand for 10 mins. (The potatoes will absorb
the water and this prevents them from absorbing all the salad

dressing.) Add the sour milk or yoghourt. Make a dressing of vinegar, oil, sugar, salt, and the chopped herbs and mix this carefully into the potato slices. Then add the mayonnaise and mix again.

NOTE. The sour milk (or yoghourt) is optional. The mayonnaise too can be left off but an extra Tbs. oil should then be used.

Russian Salad. For 4

2 medium cooked beetroots
½ lb. other cooked root vegetables such as carrots, turnips, parsnips
1 small chopped onion

1 medium apple, chopped
2 gherkins
4–5 Tbs. French Dressing or Vinaigrette (page 171)

Cut all the peeled vegetables, including the beetroots and the apple, neatly into small cubes. Make the dressing of all the other ingredients and mix well with the vegetables. This salad can be served immediately or after a few hours.

Russian Eggs. For 4

Potato Salad (see above)
4 hard-boiled eggs
1 cup mayonnaise

2 medium tomatoes
2 gherkins
1 small lettuce

Wash the lettuce and place the separated leaves on a shallow salad bowl or dish. Place the potato salad on top, leaving an outer edge of lettuce leaves visible. Peel and halve the eggs and place them on top of the potato salad. Pour the mayonnaise over so that most of it remains on top of the eggs. Cut the tomatoes and gherkins in strips or quarters and decorate the dish with them.

Marrow Salad. For 4

1 small cooked marrow
1 Tbs. chopped herbs such as parsley, chives, chervil, tarragon

1 small chopped onion or 2 spring onions
2 chopped gherkins
4–5 Tbs. vinaigrette

Cut the cooked marrow into cubes (about ½ inch). Make a dressing of all the other ingredients and mix it with the marrow cubes, taking care not to break them.

Spaghetti Salad. For 4

4 oz. spaghetti	2–3 gherkins chopped
1 cooked carrot	1 Tbs. chopped parsley
1 tomato	1 tsp. sugar
1 chopped onion or	1 tsp. salt (optional)
2 spring onions	4 Tbs. mayonnaise

Cook the spaghetti as on page 125 and cut into 2-inch lengths, the carrots and tomato into small cubes. Mix the spaghetti with all the other ingredients, except the mayonnaise which is added last. Mix again and let the dish stand for an hour or so.

Vegetable Rice Salad. For 4

Exactly as previous recipe but use rice instead of spaghetti.

Fruit and vegetable juices

There is hardly anything more health-giving and more easily digested than freshly made fruit and vegetable juices. They are invaluable for special diets, for convalescence, and just for sheer enjoyment. They are excellent as part of any meal and for something special at a cocktail party. The bottled and canned variety, good as a few products are, are no match for the home-made product.

How to Make

By Hand. No machine is needed for small quantities. Soft fruits, including tomatoes, should be cut into small pieces and leaf vegetables chopped finely. Then wrap them in a cheese cloth or a piece of any other coarsely woven material and squeeze it or twist both ends to get the juices out. Hard fruit and vegetables are first finely grated and then treated in the same way. This process is simpler than most people imagine; it is even quicker for small quantities than rigging up a machine and cleaning it later.

Screw Press. For larger quantities the old-fashioned screw press (used for making wine) is still the most effective extractor but cannot be worked continuously. The size of each batch depends obviously on the size of the press. The press must be fixed or have two people to work it. But it can be used for *all* types of fruit and vegetables.

Mincer-type Press. This uses the well-known mincer mechanism in reverse. The material (soft fruit whole, hard fruit grated) is not pushed forward as in a mincer but squeezed back through a very small, adjustable aperture where it comes out as fairly dry residue, having given up most of its liquid during the process; this liquid comes out at the front. This is an excellent method xx=good method   x=acceptable   o=not recommended

	Hand	Mincer	Electric	Possible Uses
Apple, dessert	o	o	xx	excellent by itself
Apple, cooking	o	o	xx	with honey
Grape	x	xx	o	excellent by itself
Pineapple	o	xx	x	delicious
Lemon, Orange, and other citrus	xx*	o	xx*	
Spinach	x	xx	o	in combination
Watercress	x	xx	o	in combination
Carrot	x	x	xx	excellent by itself and in combination
Beetroot	xx	x	xx	quite tasty by itself, better in combination
Other root vegetables	x	o	xx	a matter of taste
Celery	o	x	xx	very strong taste, better in combination
Tomato	x	xx	o	excellent by itself, and in combination

* Use ordinary lemon squeezer; some electric extractors have a special attachment for citrus fruit.

for very soft material (grapes, tomatoes) and can be worked as a continuous process.

Electric Juice Extractors. They usually work on the centrifugal principle. They are not cheap, but for frequent use provide the easiest and cleanest method. They are particularly useful for all hard fruit and vegetables, because they combine the shredding and extracting process in one operation. You just push the vegetable or fruit in, and the juice comes out at the spout. The only disadvantage is that after a time the centrifuge (which works like a spin-dryer) gets clogged up with the residue, particularly easy with grape or tomato skins, and it has to be cleaned before the extraction goes on.*

The table opposite shows which process is the most suitable for the fruit and vegetables most commonly used for juice. The screw press method is omitted from the table as this somewhat cumbersome machine is not an ordinary household article, but if it is available it can be used, as mentioned above, for all types of raw material.

As indicated in the table most juices can be taken without any addition. But sometimes they taste better if slightly diluted and/or with a little lemon juice, sugar, or honey added. Finely chopped parsley can also be added to vegetable juices.

Some interesting and tasty combinations are given below.

$$1 \text{ glass} = \tfrac{1}{4} \text{ pint.}$$

Carrot Milk

   1 glass carrot juice plus 1 Tbs. thin cream or milk.

Carrot Milk Shake

   $\tfrac{3}{4}$ glass carrot juice, $\tfrac{1}{4}$ glass milk, 1 tsp. honey, mixed in liquidizer, or whisked.

Carrot with Lemon (or Orange)

   1 glass carrot juice, 1 tsp. lemon juice or 1 Tbs. orange juice.

Carrot and Beetroot

   Equal amounts.

Carrot and Watercress

   Two-thirds carrot juice, one-third juice of watercress.

Carrot, Beetroot, and Spinach

   One-third of each.

---

* A new version of this has just come on the market. It can be worked continuously.

Beetroot with Lemon (or Orange)

1 glass beetroot juice (slightly diluted, if desired), with 1 tsp. lemon juice or 1 Tbs. orange juice.

Beetroot and Spinach

Equal amounts.

Spinach and Orange

1 glass spinach juice (slightly diluted, if desired) with 1 Tbs. orange juice added.

Spinach Milk

1 glass spinach juice with 1 Tbs. thin cream or milk.

Celery and Beetroot

Equal amounts (slightly diluted, if desired) with a few drops of lemon juice added.

Lemon Egg Whip. For 2

1 egg, juice of 1 lemon, 2 tsp. sugar or honey, all whipped together (a liquidizer can be used).

Orange Milk

1 glass milk with a little sugar and honey into which little by little the juice of 1 orange is whipped.

Lemon Milk

As previous recipe with 2 tsp. sugar or honey and the juice of $\frac{1}{2}$ lemon.

Fruit Yoghourt

$\frac{1}{2}$ cup yoghourt or sour milk   2 Tbs. chopped apple, pear,
$\frac{1}{2}$ cup ordinary milk   and orange, and/or mashed
$\frac{1}{2}$ tsp. sugar or honey   raspberries, strawberries

Whip together or use liquidizer.

Tomato Juice with Lemon

The juice of $\frac{1}{2}$ lemon to one glass of tomato juice.

Tomato Carrot Juice
Equal quantities of tomato and carrot juice.

Tomato Watercress Juice
Equal quantities of tomato and watercress juice.

Tomato Spinach Juice
Two-thirds tomato juice, one-third spinach juice.

Sweets

As space in this handbook is limited and as most ordinary sweets are vegetarian anyhow, there is no need to repeat here what the reader will know already or find in ordinary cookery books. However, some special sweets – not so well known – are given here; they will prove to be particularly useful for a raw vegetable and fruit diet; they are very popular for everyday use; and most are quickly made.

When making sweets for strict vegetarians note that gelatine (most jelly powders and crystals contain this) is made from animal bones; but good vegetable jelling agents such as agar-agar are available in health food stores. Suet puddings can easily be made vegetarian by substituting vegetable fat (Trex, Suenut) for animal fat.

*

Ambrosia. For 4

2 oz. rolled oats
1 cup cornflakes
½ oz. grated nuts
1½ oz. nuts, cut or coarsely grated

1 oz. fat or butter
2 oz. sugar or honey
1½ oz. sultanas and/or raisins
½ pt thin cream

Melt the fat in a strong, very clean frying pan, add the oats and ½ oz. grated nuts and roast over low heat until slightly brown, stirring from time to time to prevent burning. Then add the sugar or honey and roast for another 3 to 5 mins., stirring all the time. Put the mixture into a bowl, add first the cornflakes, then the other nuts, and lastly the sultanas and raisins. Mix well and cool. Serve with the cream.

Variations. (1) Instead of cream, serve it with one of the following: Coconut Sauce (page 173), Banana Sauce (page 172), Apple Sauce (page 172). (2) Chocolate Ambrosia. Exactly as

above recipe with the addition of 1 Tbs. grated or flaked chocolate well mixed in. (3) The amount of nuts can be reduced or
they can be entirely omitted but more oats and cornflakes
should then be used.

Apricot Sweet. For 4

4 oz. dried apricots	1 pt. milk
1 Tbs. honey	1 tsp. lemon juice (optional)

Wash the apricots in warm water and cut them in quarters.
Warm the milk a little and dissolve the honey in it. Pour over
the apricots and let it cool. The lemon juice can be added to
taste. Let the sweet stand for 12 hours before serving.

Bircher (Apple) Müesli. For 1

1 Tbs. oat flakes or oat meal	1 Tbs. sweet condensed milk* or 1 cup ordinary milk
1 Tbs. lemon juice	with 1 Tbs. honey
1 large apple	1 Tbs. grated nuts

The prepared, so-called 'quick' oats need not be soaked; otherwise soak the oats or oatmeal for about 12 hours (overnight) in
3 Tbs. water. Mix the lemon juice and milk together and pour
over the oats. Wash or peel the apple, take off the stalk and top,
and grate it on a special 'Bircher' or similar grater into the mixture, stirring occasionally to prevent the apple from browning.
Top with grated nuts and serve at once.

Variations. (1) Yoghourt and honey can be used instead of
milk and honey. (2) Strawberry Müesli, Raspberry Müesli, Red
Currant Müesli, etc., are made by the addition of these soft
fruits, but note that apple is always included as the base.

Carrot Almond Sweet. For 2

1 medium carrot	2 Tbs. milk
1½ Tbs. ground almonds	1 tsp. lemon juice
1 Tbs. cornflakes	1 tsp. sugar (brown)

Soak the cornflakes in the milk, add the other ingredients (the

* When Dr Bircher-Benner invented this dish, ordinary milk was not
considered safe.

carrots very finely grated). Mix well and stand for about 20 to 30 mins., when the mixture should be quite firm. If the carrot is very watery, use less milk or more cornflakes. Serve with whipped cream.

Carrot Fig Sweet. For 2
See Carrots, Figs, and Apples (page 180).

Chocolate Cream. For 1

1 Tbs. grated or flaked chocolate	1 Tbs. grated nuts
	1½ Tbs. whipped cream

Just mix all ingredients together.

Filled Apple Rings. For 2

1 large dessert apple	2 Tbs. grated nuts
1 Tbs. cream cheese	1 Tbs. corn or oatflakes
3 Tbs. milk	1 Tbs. sugar or honey
2 Tbs. chopped raisins	some whole nuts

Wash and dry the apple, take out the core, and cut the apple into thick rings. The filling is made by mixing first the milk and cream cheese to a smooth paste and then mixing in the sugar, grated nuts, raisins, and flakes. Place the apple rings on a plate and fill the core hole with this mixture. Garnish with a whole nut on each ring. If the dish is not served at once, paint the apple rings with lemon juice to prevent browning.

Filled Apricots. For 1

2 fresh apricots	1 tsp. vanilla sugar
1 Tbs. whipped cream	a little grated chocolate
½ Tbs. grated nuts	

Wash the apricots, cut them in half and take out the stones. Make a mixture of all the other ingredients. Fill the apricots and serve on some green leaves.

Filled Peach. For 1
Same as previous recipe with 1 peach instead of the 2 apricots.

Fruit Cream. For 4

1 small apple	4 oz. curd cheese or
1 pear	cream cheese
4–6 cherries	2 Tbs. milk
½ orange	2 Tbs. sugar
a few grapes or similar	1 Tbs. lemon juice
combination of fruit	1 Tbs. grated nuts

Mix the cheese, milk, and lemon juice to a smooth cream and add the sugar. Cut or chop the fruit into very small pieces, mix with the cream and serve in glass dishes topped with the grated nuts.

Fruit Medley. For 4

6 oz. dried fruit such as	2 Tbs. grated nuts
stoned prunes, dates, apricots,	1 oz. desiccated or grated
sultanas	coconut
1 small apple	

Put the washed dried fruit and the apple through a mincer. Mix in the grated nuts. Grease a baking sheet slightly with oil and spread the mixture on to it. Press down and sprinkle with the coconut. Let stand for an hour or two. Then cut into squares. Can be served with whipped cream.

Fruit Truffles. For 4

6 oz. dried fruit as previous	2 Tbs. cream or milk
recipe	1 oz. ground almonds
2 oz. grated nuts	some desiccated coconut or
2 oz. cornflakes or	chocolate vermicelli
other flakes or cake crumbs	

Mince the dried fruit and mix it well with the flakes, nuts, and milk. Let it stand for an hour. Then make little balls between your hands and roll some in ground almonds, some in desiccated coconut, and others in chocolate vermicelli.

Fruit Mélange. For 4

6 oz. dried fruit as in	2 Tbs. honey
Fruit Medley	1 tsp. lemon juice
1 pt milk	

Wash the dried fruit and cut it into small pieces or strips. Mix
the milk with the honey and lemon juice and pour this over the
fruit. Mix again and let it stand for 12 hours (overnight).

Fruit Salad. For 2

1 apple	a few grapes or plums and/or
1 orange	any other fruit in season
1 banana	1 Tbs. sugar or honey
	2 Tbs. water

Cut all fruit into pieces of similar size. Grapes and cherries
are best halved and stoned. Mix well with the sugar (or honey)
and water. Let it stand for anything between half an hour and
two hours. It can be served with a topping of grated nuts or
whipped cream or both.

Fruit Trifle (uncooked). For 4

1½ cups cornflakes	2 small bananas
2 Tbs. milk	a few grapes (optional)
2 Tbs. brown sugar	½ pt cream for whipping
2 medium apples	

Crush the cornflakes, mix them with the sugar and put this into
the bottom of a pie dish or bowl. Grate the apples, mash the
bananas, and mix both well together with the milk. Then
spread this mixture on top of the cornflakes. Cover this with a
layer of whipped cream and decorate (optional) with the grapes.
Let it stand for an hour and/or chill in a refrigerator.

Pineapple Rings. For 4

1 small fresh pineapple	½ pt cream for whipping
2 Tbs. grated nuts	

Top and tail the pineapple and cut it into four thick slices. Cut
out the fleshy part of the pineapple so as not to break the skin
which will be used as a ring to hold the finished Pineapple
Cream. Chop the pineapple and mix with the whipped cream
and nuts. Put this mixture back into the rings and serve.

Russian Cream. For 4

6 oz. curd cheese or cream cheese	2 oz. sugar
½ pt milk	2 oz. raisins and sultanas mixed
1 tsp. lemon juice	2 oz. grated nuts

Beat the cheese and milk to a thick cream, add all the other ingredients, and mix well. A little grated lemon rind can be added.

Stuffed Dates

These are simply made by washing the dates first in warm water, then stoning them and stuffing each with a Brazil nut kernel, a walnut or two hazelnut kernels. Small pieces of marzipan are also useful for stuffing.

Continental Apple Tart. For 6

Crust	*Filling*
3 oz. margarine or fat	2 large cooking apples (¾ lb.)
3 oz. sugar	1 Tbs. crumbs (bread or cake)
6 oz. flour	3 oz. sugar
1 egg	1 oz. sultanas
1 Tbs. milk	

Sift the flour and add 3 oz. sugar. Mix in the margarine with fingertips until the mixture resembles breadcrumbs. Break the egg in a cup, beat slightly and add to the mixture (but keep a little egg for painting the top of the tart later), finally add the milk. Knead this into a thick dough and let it stand for at least ½ hour. Then roll out half the pastry into a round and line a greased and floured sandwich tin or baking tin of about 8-inch diameter. Bake blind (for explanation see page 143) for 10 to 15 mins. in a fairly hot oven (400–425°, Reg. 6–7). In the meantime prepare the filling. Peel and core the apples, cut them into thin slices and wash the sultanas. Then take the blind baked pastry out of the oven, put in the filling: first a layer of breadcrumbs or cake crumbs, then the sliced apples, then the sultanas, and finally 2½ oz. sugar. Roll out the remainder of the pastry into another round. Cover the filling with it, pressing down the sides firmly. Paint the top with the little left-over egg (water would do) and sprinkle the remaining ½ oz. sugar on top. Bake for another 30 to 40 mins., same temperature.

This is a very useful sweet as it can be served hot or cold, with or without (whipped) cream. Left-over tart makes an attractive pastry with tea or coffee.

Stuffed Apples. For 4

4 medium or large apples	½ Tbs. butter or less
2 Tbs. currants or sultanas	½ cup apple juice or water
3 Tbs. cream	grated peel of ½ lemon
2½ Tbs. sugar	2 Tbs. grated nuts

Wash the apples, take out the core, and make an incision round the apple just cutting the skin. Mix the grated nuts with the currants, cream, 2 Tbs. sugar, and add the grated lemon peel. This mixture is then put into the centre of the apples. Put the apples into a deep fireproof dish (or pie dish). Dab the butter on the apples and sprinkle the remaining ½ Tbs. sugar on top. Pour the apple juice or water into the dish and bake for 20 to 30 mins. in a hot oven (400–425°, Reg. 6–7). Serve hot with or without cream.

Rhubarb Slices. For 4

4 slices wholemeal bread	4 oz. sugar
¾ lb. rhubarb	3 Tbs. cream
1 oz. butter	

Trim top and bottom of the rhubarb and wash (do not peel). Cut it into pieces of about 1 inch. Put them together with the sugar (no water) into a saucepan and stew over low heat carefully, stirring just a little at the beginning. The rhubarb pieces should be soft after 10 to 15 mins., but should not fall to pieces. Cool. Melt the butter in a frying pan and fry the bread until it is light brown on both sides. Arrange the pieces of rhubarb neatly on the fried bread. Whip the cream and garnish the slices with it before serving.

This sweet can also be served hot; in this case, of course, the rhubarb has to be kept warm.

Fruit Charlotte. For 4

6 slices wholemeal bread	3 oz. butter
¾ lb. fresh fruit (apples,	juice and rind of 1 lemon or
plums, cherries, etc.)	orange
3 oz. sugar	

Wash, peel and cut the fruit (cherries or plums to be stoned). Melt the butter and dip the bread into it until it is well covered. Line a pie dish with four slices of this bread and fill it up with the fruit, the sugar, and the juice and rind of the lemon (or orange). Cover with the remaining two slices of bread, and bake in a moderate oven (350°, Reg. 4) for about 45 mins. When ready, sprinkle a little sugar over it and serve hot with or without cream.

Fruit Delight. For 4

This is the famous Danish Rød Grøde or German Rote Grütze.

1½ lb. strawberries, red cur-	4 Tbs. cornflour
rants, raspberries, or a	7 oz. sugar
mixture of these	1 gill cream (optional)
1½ pt water	1 lemon

Wash and prepare the fruit (hull the strawberries and raspberries, strip the currants). Boil the fruit in ½ pt water until quite soft. Strain (keep the water). Then rub the fruit through a sieve, add the fruit water and the other pint of water, then the sugar and the rind and juice of the lemon, and bring to the boil. Mix the cornflour well with a little cold water and pour this into the boiling fruit mixture. Cook slowly for about 10 mins., stirring all the time. Then take off the flame and pour the mixture into a pre-warmed bowl; it looks best in a glass bowl. Let cool and serve cold, if desired with whipped or thin cream.

Lemon Soufflé with Lemon Sauce. For 4

Soufflé

1½ oz. butter or margarine	4 eggs
1½ oz. flour	3 oz. sugar
6 Tbs. milk (1½ gill)	rind of 1 lemon

Melt the butter in a saucepan and add the flour. Stir well and when both are blended add the milk and simmer for 5 or 6 mins., stirring all the time. Then let it cool a little and add the sugar and lemon rind. Mix in the egg yolks one by one. Whisk the egg whites separately and fold this in lightly with a metal spoon. Pour the mixture into a pie dish (or soufflé dish) but as the soufflé will rise to double its original size, the pie dish should be only half full. Bake for 30 mins. in a moderate oven (375°, Reg. 4). Serve at once.

Sauce
1½ cup water   2 oz. sugar
1½ lemons   2 tsp. cornflour

Grate off the rind of the lemons, squeeze out the juice. Mix this with the rind, the water, and the sugar. Bring to boil. Mix the cornflour with a little cold water and add to the boiling mixture. Cook over gentle heat for 5 to 8 mins., stirring all the time. Serve hot with the soufflé.

Sandwich spreads and cocktail tit-bits

When you are preparing items for a cocktail party or buffet meal bear in mind that normally no cutlery is provided for your guests which means that each item should be small enough to be eaten at a bite, even if some of them are provided with cocktail sticks. Colourful (and tasty) sandwich spreads should not be hidden, but spread on open sandwiches (Swedish *smörsgasbord* fashion) cut very small, or on open bridge roll halves. Capers or slices of tiny gherkins are excellent for decorating these open sandwiches and give an extra piquant flavour. Other useful decorative items are: small pieces of tomato, chopped up white of hard-boiled egg, and dabs of mayonnaise.

For special Health Cocktails see page 205.

SANDWICH SPREADS

All these spreads contain butter (or margarine) which should be mixed well with the other ingredients.

Mock Crab (Red)

2 oz. butter
1 tsp. finely grated onion

1 oz. grated cheese
1 tsp. tomato purée

Herb Butter (Green)

2 oz. butter
pinch of yeast extract

1 Tbs. finely chopped herbs such as cress, parsley, chives, spring onion (green part)

Marmite Spread (Brown)

2 oz. butter
1 small tsp. yeast extract

Mix well to a smooth brown cream. If it is streaky, continue mixing with a fork.

Hazelnut Spread (White)

2 oz. butter	¼ tsp. finely chopped onion
1 oz. ground hazelnuts	(optional)

Egg Spread (Yellow)

2 oz. butter	2 tsp. mayonnaise
2 hard-boiled eggs	1 tsp. chopped onion
(finely chopped)	½ tsp. chopped parsley

COCKTAIL PASTRIES

Caraway Seed Biscuits

4 oz. flour	1 Tbs. milk or water
2 oz. butter	1 egg yolk (optional)
1 small whole egg (optional)	caraway seeds

Mix the butter (cut in pieces) into the flour with your finger tips until the mixture resembles breadcrumbs. Add salt (if desired), the whole egg, and milk (or water). If no eggs are used add 2 to 3 Tbs. water. Mix to a stiff dough. Let it rest in a cool place for one or two hours. Roll out and cut in strips with a pastry wheel or into shapes with suitable pastry cutters (petits fours cutters are useful). Place on a greased and floured baking sheet, paint with the egg yolk (optional) and sprinkle some caraway seeds on top. Bake in a moderate oven (350–375°, Reg. 4–5) for 15 to 20 mins. These quantities give about 6 oz. of biscuits.

Cheese Biscuits

6 oz. flour	4 oz. grated cheese
4 oz. butter	1 egg yolk (optional)

Mix the flour and butter as in the previous recipe, add the cheese and knead to a dough. This will take a little time as it will at first be rather crumbly, but do not add any liquid. Let it rest in a cool place for ½ to 1 hour. Roll it out on a floured board (the dough may still be a little sticky which cannot be helped if a really good end product is desired), cut into strips or shapes as described in the previous recipe and paint with the whisked egg yolk. Bake in a moderate oven (350°, Reg. 4) for 15 to 20 mins. The biscuits should be very light brown. Being very light and crisp they break easily and should be handled carefully. These quantities make about ¾ lb. of biscuits.

Filled Savoury Éclairs

Make Choux Pastry (page 145). Using a plain round nozzle, pipe on to a floured baking sheet in very small balls (not bigger than 1 inch) or strips 1 to 1½ inches long, and bake in moderate oven (350°, Reg. 4) for 25 mins., or until just beginning to brown. When cold cut in half and fill with one of the following:

Egg Filling. Chop 1 to 3 hard-boiled eggs finely and mix with a little chopped onion, watercress, parsley, lemon juice, and mayonnaise, but do not let it get too stiff.

Cream Cheese Filling. Cream Cheese Sauce (page 173).

Mayonnaise Fillings. Plain mayonnaise, with perhaps a little beetroot juice or spinach juice added for colouring. Alternatively add finely chopped gherkins, olives, parsley, and chives (for Mayonnaise Piquante).

The éclairs can also be topped with a little coloured mayonnaise and put on cocktail sticks.

Pastry Boats and Baskets

Make Short Pastry (page 143). Roll it out thinly, press it into small boat-form baking tins, cut off any surplus pastry round the edges and bake them in a moderate to hot oven (400°, Reg. 6) for about 15 mins. Let them cool and take them out of the tins. Fill with mayonnaise (see previous recipe) or cream cheese. Use half a thin lemon or cucumber slice as a sail and a cocktail stick as mast.

For baskets use small round (1½ inch) baking forms. Bake and fill as in previous recipe. Use a half-round of lemon rind as handle. These look especially attractive if the filling is topped with a tiny sprig of parsley, or a small slice of olive.

Paulette Bits

Prepare a few slices of Mushroom Paulette Toast (page 166).

Cut them into 1-inch squares, making sure that each square has
a slice of mushroom on top. Garnish with anything to hand such
as bits of tomato, gherkin or olive. Put a cocktail stick through
each square.

Tomato Rare Bits

2 rounds dry toast
2 large tomatoes
  (or 4 small ones)
1 tsp. tomato purée
½ oz. fat

2 Tbs. Cheese Sauce (page 97)
1 oz. grated cheese
2 small gherkins
4 black olives

Cut the tomatoes into thick slices and fry in the fat for two
minutes (they should not be quite soft). Mix the cheese sauce
with the tomato purée and about half the fried tomato slices.
Spread this mixture evenly on the toast and top with the grated
cheese and the rest of the tomato slices, cut in halves or quarters.
Put under a hot grill until the cheese has melted and the tomatoes
are soft. When cool, cut into small squares, making sure there is
a piece of tomato on each, and serve on cocktail sticks garnished
as in the previous recipe with the black olives and gherkins.

Pumpernickel Layer Bits

3 slices of pumpernickel or
  other black rye bread
2 slices brown or white bread
  not too fresh, thinly sliced

1 oz. butter
2 oz. cream cheese

Butter all five slices of bread. Spread a slice of buttered pumpernickel with cream cheese, and cover it with a slice of white
bread, buttered side down. Spread the top of this with cream
cheese and cover with another pumpernickel slice, buttered side
down again, repeat until the third slice of pumpernickel is placed
on top, buttered side down. Press the bread firmly together and
cut it with a very sharp large kitchen knife into 1-inch squares
(or smaller). Serve on cocktail sticks.

OTHER COCKTAIL TIT-BITS

Filled Celery

a few good celery sticks
chopped parsley
a little cream cheese

tomato purée
pinch of paprika pepper

Cut the celery into 1½-inch lengths. Mix some of the cream cheese with the tomato purée. (If another colour is required, mix some more with a little spinach juice.) Fill the hollow side of the celery sticks with any of these, and decorate the white and green filling with a little paprika, the red with chopped parsley.

Vegetarian Cocktail Sausages

Use any of the rissole recipes (pages 135–6) but shape into very small sausages (say, as thick as the little finger, but half the length). Instead of covering them with egg and breadcrumbs roll them in flour and fry in deep fat. Serve on cocktail sticks.

Salted Almonds

½ lb. shelled almonds
salt

4 oz. butter or
4 Tbs. oil

Blanch the almonds by pouring boiling water over them to remove any remaining brown skins. Let them stand for a few minutes, and then squeeze out the kernels. Dry them on a towel. Melt the butter, add the almonds, turn them to coat them well with the butter and fry them over a moderate heat, turning them again from time to time. As soon as they are light brown, take them off the flame, place them on a sheet of blotting or kitchen paper, and sprinkle them with salt before they get cold. Left-over salted almonds can be kept for several weeks in a screw-topped jar.

Filled Eggs

4 hard-boiled eggs
2 Tbs. mayonnaise (page 171)
a little lemon juice

½ tsp. chopped herbs
(parsley, chives, etc.)
mustard and salt (optional)

Shell the eggs and cut them in half lengthwise. Take the yolks out carefully. Mash these with all the other ingredients, and put them back into the egg-white halves. Garnish with a little piece of tomato or a tiny sprig of parsley.

Filled Cucumber

See page 186.

Filled Tomatoes

See page 195. Use small tomatoes.

Cream Cheese Balls

4 oz. cream cheese	1 Tbs. cornflakes or
1 oz. ground almonds	fine breadcrumbs
1 oz. ground nuts	

Crush the cornflakes to a fine powder and mix with the cream cheese and ground almonds. Form into small balls. Cover them with ground nuts.

Menu suggestions

Planning the menu for her family is one of the housewife's most important tasks; health and happiness may depend on it. The suggestions here are meant as a general guide only, as the availability of vegetables, personal taste, and the size of your purse also have to be taken into consideration. Items are of course interchangeable: for instance Mashed Potatoes can be given instead of Boiled Potatoes, or a leaf vegetable, say spinach, changed for another, say cabbage. In fact we strongly recommend you to substitute a salad for a cooked vegetable dish as often as possible, and not only during the summer.

Balance

The provision of sufficient protein often worries people changing to a vegetarian diet, although in the Western world the average adult's consumption of protein is too high rather than too low. However, the main courses suggested in this section take care of this quite adequately, and *any* soup, sweet, or salad may be given as an additional course or courses. Only occasionally where we have put an asterisk (*) might it be advisable to provide some extra protein, particularly if you are catering for growing children. This is easily done by choosing as a further course a rich soup or sweet (see the appropriate sections in this book): rich in protein, that is, containing either egg, milk, cream, cheese, or nuts. Another way to increase protein is to serve grated cheese as an addition to soups or vegetables, or cream cheese or nuts in salads.

Menus

We have sub-divided the menu suggestions as follows:
    In the first part we give 'economy' menus, and these take into

account simplicity of preparation too. The second part contains suggestions only slightly more elaborate for the average household. In the third part sample menus for festive occasions are given, and finally in the fourth part there are examples for an 'uncooked' diet.

The first two parts are sub-divided again according to seasons. These are, in Great Britain's temperate climate: (a) about August to February, the season of plenty; then (b) March to June when vegetables begin to get scarce and when we have to rely to some extent on pulses (peas, beans, lentils) and imported frozen, and tinned vegetables until (c) in June/July the young vegetables make their first appearance.

1. *Economy Menus*

Examples of the main course only are given. For additional courses see under 'Balance' above.

(a) *August to February*

Creamed Leeks with Poached Egg and Baked Potatoes

Cauliflower au Gratin with Jacket Potatoes

*Stuffed Cabbage Dish with Steamed Carrots (and Butter)

Pease Pudding and Steamed Brussels Sprouts

Risotto with Grated Cheese and Braised Onions

Cabbage in Tomato Sauce with Cheese Potatoes

*Fried Sauerkraut with Mashed Potatoes

Brussels Sprouts in Cheese Sauce with Carrots Vichy and Jacket Potatoes

Bauernfrühstück (Farmer's Breakfast) with Creamed Swedes

Lentil Pudding with Carrots and Celery à la Crème

Creamed Spinach with Poached (or Fried) Egg and Bircher Potatoes

*Vegetable Hot Pot served with Shredded Carrot (or other) Salad

Vegetable Rissole with Leeks au Gratin

Cauliflower with Hollandaise Sauce (or au Gratin) and Jacket Potatoes

*Brussels Sprouts and Carrots à la Crème with Potato Dumplings

Tomato Eggs with Creamed Turnips

Celery au Gratin with Potatoes Lyonnaise
Nut Rissole with Tomato Sauce and Braised Onions
*Macaroni Stew with Creamed Spinach
Cheese Pancake and Mashed Swedes with Fried Onions
*Baked Tomato Rice with Creamed Jerusalem Artichokes
Semolina Pudding with Grated Cheese and Steamed Brussels Sprouts
*Bavarian Red Cabbage with Bircher (or Baked) Potatoes

(*b*) *March to June*
Spaghetti au Gratin with Beetroot Ragoût
Pease Pudding with Steamed Carrots and Scrambled Egg
*Steamed Swedes with Onion Sauce and Fried Potatoes
*Carrot-Onion-Potato Casserole and Baked Potatoes
*Bubble and Squeak with Parsnips Béchamel
Lentil Pie with Creamed Mixed Greens
Egg Spaghetti with White Cabbage and Caraway Seeds

(*c*) *June/July*
Creamed Broad Beans (with the pods) and Baked Potatoes
Stewed Young Carrots with Italian Potatoes
Green Cabbage (Spring Greens) with Cheese Beignets and Jacket
    Potatoes
Filled (any filling) Pancake with Broad Bean Stew
*Macaroni Rissole with Carrots and Peas à la Crème
Spinach Florentine and Jacket Potatoes
Nut Rissole with Steamed Green Peas (and Mint) and New Jacket
    Potatoes
Mixed Vegetable Dish with Eggburgers
Dhal, Kedgeree, or Pease Pudding with Green Cabbage (Spring
    Greens) in Tomato Sauce
Stuffed Young Marrow with Mashed Potatoes
Vegetable Rissole with Cauliflower in Cheese Sauce
Marrow-Tomato-Onion Casserole with Chipped Potatoes

Semolina Cheese Pudding with Young Turnips and Turnip Tops à la Crème

Lentil Rissole with Carrots and Peas Béchamel

Leaf Spinach with Scrambled Egg and Plain Rice

Vegetable Marrow au Gratin with Sauté Potatoes

Runner Beans and White Beans with Baked Tomato Rice

2. *Menus for the Average Family*

Again only the main course is given. For additional courses see under 'Balance' (page 225).

(a) *August to February*

*Tomato Onion Pancake with Steamed Brussels Sprouts and Roast Potatoes

Chicory Egg Dish with Mashed Carrots and Jacket Potatoes

Rice Croquettes with Gravy served with Leaf Spinach and Leeks au Gratin

Mushroom Omelette with Steamed Cauliflower and Mashed Potatoes

Vegetable Pie and Gravy with Jacket Potatoes. Tomato Salad

Semolina Gnocchi with Carrots Sauté and Jerusalem Artichokes with Pimento Sauce

Nut Rissoles and Gravy with Red Cabbage and Creamed Chestnuts

Cheese Soufflé with Creamed Curly Kale and Baked Potatoes

*Bavarian Dumplings with Horseradish Sauce served with Fried Sauerkraut. Endive or Lettuce Salad

Tomato Oat Cakes with Steamed Brussels Sprouts and Italian Potatoes

*Vegetable Chop Suey with Plain Rice and Curry Sauce

Celery au Gratin with Steamed Carrots and Potato Cakes

Spanish Egg Spaghetti with Stewed Green Cabbage. Beetroot Salad

Leek Pie with Cheese Sauce served with Leaf Spinach and Grilled Tomatoes

Cheese Beignets with Mixed Vegetable Dish (Leipziger Allerlei) and Mashed Potatoes

(b) *March to June*

Mushroom Rice with Cabbage à la Crème and Roast Potato es

Cornish Pasties with Gravy served with Steamed Broccoli, Celery and Apple Salad

Baked Beans in Tomato Sauce with Stewed Turnips and Cheese Potatoes

Mushroom Soufflé with Creamed Spinach and Boiled Potatoes

*Brown Lentil Stew with Potato and Lettuce Salad

Ravioli with Tomato Sauce served with Creamed Celery and Carrot Potatoes

Yorkshire Pudding and Gravy with Creamed Mixed Greens and Bircher Potatoes

*Red Cabbage with Apple Fritters served with Stewed Celery and Jacket Potatoes

Tomato Omelette with Steamed Cauliflower and Swiss Potatoes

Pease Pudding with Creamed Carrots. Cabbage (or other) Salad

Sauerkraut Potato Dish (Pommes Mousseline à la Choucroute) with Creamed Spinach

(c) *June/July*

Rice Croquettes and Cheese Sauce with Steamed Young Carrots. Green Salad

Tomato Soufflé with Young Broad Beans (with pods) à la Béchamel and New Jacket Potatoes

Cheese Puffs with Peas and Mint. New Baked Potatoes

Spaghetti Neapolitana with Young Turnips sautés. Tomato Cress Salad

Young Carrots and Peas à la Crème. Sauté Potatoes and Scrambled Egg

Fresh Asparagus with Hollandaise Sauce. Creamed Mixed Greens and New Jacket Potatoes

Curried Egg and Plain Rice. Steamed French Beans

Onion Tart and Creamed Spinach. Shredded Young Carrot Salad with Lettuce and/or Cress

Yorkshire Pudding with Runner Beans Béchamel and New Boiled Potatoes

3. *Some Menus for Festive Occasions**

Half Grapefruit

Egg and Mushroom Roll with
  Mushroom Sauce
Carrots and Peas à la crème
Mashed Potatoes

Fruit Trifle

*

Clear Vegetable Broth Garni

Corn Pancakes
Ratatouille Niçoise
Mashed Potatoes

Salad

Chocolate Ambrosia

*

Mushroom Cream Soup

Stuffed Aubergines (or Stuffed
  Marrow) with Gravy
Green Peas with Butter Sauce
Cheese Potatoes

Carrot Almond Sweet

*

Cold Orange Soup

Mushroom Omelette
Asparagus with Sauce
  Hollandaise
Braised Celery
New Potatoes

Pineapple Rings

*

Carrot Juice with Lemon

Pizza Napolitana
Spinach à la Béchamel
Steamed Aubergines

Salad

Fruit Mélange with Cream

*

Cold Strawberry Soup

Stuffed Pepper with Tomato
  Sauce
Creamed Spinach
Potato Cakes

Russian Cream

*

Tomato Juice

Nut Roast
Bavarian Red Cabbage
Mashed Potatoes and Onion
  Rings

Apricot Sweet

*

For Christmas:

Asparagus Cream Soup

Cheese Soufflé
Brussels Sprouts with Chestnuts
Carrots Vichy
Chipped Potatoes

Christmas Pudding or
Fruit Salad

Filled Celery and other Cocktail
  Bits

* Cheese and biscuits, coffee, cocktail tit-bits etc. can of course be
used to round off each meal.

4. *Menus for an Uncooked Diet*

The general rule is to start with a fruit or vegetable juice as an appetizer, then follow with a large salad plate consisting of a root vegetable, a leaf vegetable, and fruit (including tomatoes and cucumber). (The salad can be served with a cooked dish such as Jacket or Baked Potatoes or a savoury dish.) Finish with an uncooked sweet.

Fruit Yoghourt
Filled Cucumber, Spinach with Tomatoes, Parsnip Mayonnaise, Lettuce and/or Cress
Stuffed Dates

Apple Juice
Tomato with Herb Sauce, Beetroot with Raisin, Cole Slaw, Lettuce and/or Cress
Russian Cream

Tomato Juice with Lemon
Apple and Date Salad, Shredded Beetroots with Horseradish Sauce, Cabbage Mayonnaise, Lettuce and/or Cress
Ambrosia with Cream

Grape Juice
Marrow and Tomato Salad, Carrots with Coconut, Celery Rémoulade, Lettuce and/or Cress
Bircher Müesli

Spinach and Tomato Juice
American Salad, Radishes with Herb Sauce, Red Cabbage Salad, Lettuce and/or Cress
Fruit Medley with Cream

Carrot and Beetroot Juice
Salade May Irwin (Tomato, Cucumber, and Spring Onions), Cauliflower with Nuts, Celery and Apple Salad, Lettuce and/or Cress
Apricot Sweet

Orange Juice

Tomato, Leek, and Apple Salad, Mixed Root Mayonnaise, Marrow Rémoulade, Lettuce and/or Cress

Pineapple Cream

Tomato Watercress Juice

Grapefruit Salad, Cauliflower and Carrots, Cucumber Salad, Lettuce and/or Cress

Chocolate Cream

Pineapple Juice

Tomato filled with Cream Cheese, Turnips with Dates, Spinach Mayonnaise, Lettuce and/or Cress

Corn Salad

Celery and Beetroot Juice

Carrot Pudding with Nut Sauce, Cabbage Mayonnaise, Tomato Salad, Lettuce and/or Cress

Fruit Cream

Orange Milk

Pumpkin with Apples, Carrots and Celery Salad, Spinach Mayonnaise, Lettuce and/or Cress

Stuffed Dates

Tomato Carrot Juice

Grape Salad, Celeriac Mayonnaise, Cabbage with Raisins, Lettuce and/or Cress

Filled Peaches

Index